THE LA
BETW

THE LANDS BETWEEN

BY JOHN S. BADEAU

FRIENDSHIP PRESS NEW YORK

All Bible quotations used in this book, except where otherwise designated, are from the Revised Standard Version, copyright, 1946 and 1952, by the Division of Christian Education of the National Council of the Churches of Christ in the United States of America.

SET IN TIMES ROMAN 10 POINT LEADED 3 POINTS. • PRINTED AND BOUND BY SOWERS PRINTING COMPANY, LEBANON, PA. • JACKETS AND PAPER COVERS BY AFFILIATED LITHOGRAPHERS, INC., NEW YORK, N. Y. • PAPER: S. D. WARREN'S OLDE STYLE WOVE • TYPOGRAPHIC DESIGN BY MARGERY W. SMITH • BINDING BY LOUISE E. JEFFERSON

Library of Congress Catalog Card Number: 58-7027

CONTENTS

PART ONE: LAND AND PEOPLE

PART TWO: STATE AND SOCIETY

PART THREE: MOSQUE AND CHURCH

MAPS

PART ONE

LAND AND PEOPLE

1

Why Is the Middle East?

❡ WHEN Abraham left Ur of the Chaldeans and wandered westward to the Great Sea, he traversed the heart of the Middle East. But he did not know it. No one in his day or for centuries thereafter would use this, or any other distinctive term, to describe the lands that lie at the eastern end of the Mediterranean. To him it was simply the "world," filled with the different peoples and nations—"the Kenites, the Kenizzites, the Kadmonites, the Hittites, the Perizzites, the Rephaims, the Amorites, the Canaanites, the Girgashites, and the Jebusites" (Genesis 15:19-21).

Abraham's simple concept was not due solely to the narrow horizons and limited geographical knowledge of the ancient world. It was also a valid, if unconscious, reflection of the basic diversity of geography and human life in the lands through which he passed. Between the head of the Persian Gulf, where Ur lay, and the banks of the Nile to which the patriarch finally came, fertile river valleys, barren desert wastes, grassy steppes, rain-drenched seacoasts, and towering mountain ranges followed one upon another. Petty kings and tribal chiefs held rule over a checkerboard of small states. Tongues, races, and religions changed with a week's caravan journey. There was little to suggest that either the lands or their people would ever be distinguished by a single regional name.

Much has happened since Abraham's day to overlay this diversity. A series of great, though vanished, empires have left dim memories of a common political destiny; the faith and practice of Islam have stamped a common pattern on personal and social life; and the Arabic language has obliterated many ancient tongues. In recent years a kinship of nationalistic resentment prevails against the West—a reaction to more than a century of European political influence and control.

Yet the variety of topography, climate, rainfall, and people is still basic and inescapable, and it is difficult, as well as misleading, to treat the area simply as a single region. Indeed, the geographer and anthropologist are hard pressed to define the Middle East in terms of their own sciences. Some even question if there *is* a Middle East at all beyond the minds and concern of diplomats.

How then did it happen that a single term came to be used for such diversity? Why was that term first "Near East" and later "Middle East?" The answer is found in history, not in geography, for the regional concept and the names used for it are the products of the West's great Age of Discovery. Until the times of Marco Polo, Dias, and da Gama, the region at and beyond the eastern seacoast of the Mediterranean was simply the East or the Levant. There the Greeks found their supreme opponent, Persia, and Alexander the Great's meteoric conquests briefly lifted the curtain on India and the Persian Gulf. In Roman days the Parthian rulers blocked Latin expansion eastward, although the empire's far-flung commerce occasionally reached India, China, and Ceylon to bring to Mediterranean markets the luxuries of Eastern lands. As Europe passed into its Dark Ages, even this casual contact was lost and the East became a region of myth and fancy, out of whose mists came the Arab caravans bringing their burdens of incense and spice.

Europe's Age of Discovery in the fifteenth and sixteenth centuries created a "new" East. Those half-forgotten lands—India, China, Japan, and the Pacific Isles—became centers of Western interest, beginning Europe's great imperial expansion. Since they were many months' journey from home and markedly different from the East that had become familiar through the Crusades, they quickly became known as the Far East or the High Levant. The old East then became the Near East or Low Levant; some called it the Nearer East—a term that is still used in Arabic.

In recent years another term has been coined—the "Middle East." Originally a British usage, this term referred to those lands that do not directly adjoin Europe (Egypt, Palestine, Turkey, Syria, Iraq, Arabia, and Iran) yet are not truly Oriental in the sense of China and Japan. Thus the old East could be neatly divided into Near, Middle, and Far, to the delight of all gazetteers. But lacking a scientific basis in geography and faced with the tenacity of established usage, this scheme has never been universally adopted. Today the terms "Near" and "Middle" East are used interchangeably, to the confusion of everyone, even the experts. The National Geographic Society still labels its maps of the area "The Lands of the Near East," while one of the outstanding organizations studying the region is named the "Middle East Institute."

Despite their conflicting usage, these names all emphasize that the area they designate owes its regional character to something that lies beyond its borders. It is because these lands, with all their natural diversities, are "near to" or "in the middle of" other regions that they are included in a single term. This means that whatever unity the Middle East has is chiefly functional. It is a unity impressed from without, not an inherent unity arising from similar geographical or social conditions. In fact there is no Middle-East-in-itself; it is always a Middle-East-in-relation-to some other part of the world.

That other part of the world is Asia, Africa, and Europe. Although these continents appear on the map as a continuous land mass, the natural barriers between them have focused major intercourse in the area where all three meet. It is this area that we call the Middle East. Broadly defined, the Middle East is that central region composed of portions of Africa, Asia, and Europe through which the traveler passes on his way from one continent to another. Like a corridor, the Middle East owes its existence mainly to its function as a passageway and connector.

More exactly, the Middle East is bound by a series of natural barriers that both separate it from, yet provide access to, its tricontinental surroundings. On the north is a chain of inland seas (Black, Caspian, Aral) linked together by forbidding mountain ranges and semi-arid steppes. On the south is the world's most extensive desert, the Sahara, which seals off the heart of Africa from the Mediterranean coast lands. On the west lies the Mediterranean Sea. On the east there is the Indian Ocean with its two arms, the Persian Gulf and the Red Sea. The region enclosed within these borders is considered the Near or Middle East.

Yet at two points these borders are not precise. From the standpoint of geography, the Nile Valley is usually taken as the western limit of the Middle East. Considered culturally, however, the area actually extends across the whole of North Africa until it meets the Atlantic Ocean on the beaches of Morocco. This cultural extension arises because the countries north of the Sahara are principally Arab in origin and dominantly Muslim in faith—a result of the Arab conquests of the seventh and eighth centuries. Thus, although facing Europe, North Africa looks eastward for its historic connections to Cairo and Damascus, the strongholds of Arab-Muslim life. The deep interest of the Arab states in the struggles of Algeria with the French is partly an expression of this sense of cultural community that binds North Africa with the Middle East rather than with its European neighbors to the north.

The other indefinite area of the Middle East lies between and beyond the Caspian and Aral Seas, on the northeast corner of the region. Here the semi-arid steppes of the trans-Caspian plains open a roadway to the heart of central Asia. It was through this area that Marco Polo traveled when he sought the court of Kublai Khan in Cathay. Afghanistan can be classified either as the southern point of central Asia, or the extreme eastern end of the Middle East. Viewed from the functional definition we have used, it really belongs to the Middle East, for the overland route to India passes across Afghanistan and down through the Khyber Pass to the plains of the Punjab.

Some would include western Pakistan in the Middle East for the same reasons as North Africa. It is true that Pakistan, especially in its northern borders, is closely related to Afghanistan in tribal life, speech, and political history. It is also true that Pakistan is Muslim in faith and so feels kinship to the heartland of Islam in the Middle East. Yet racially and historically Pakistan is part of the Indian subcontinent and does not look to Damascus and Cairo the way North Africa does. Its major political problems lie eastward with India, not westward with Europe, and in all but faith it is essentially Indian.

The tricontinental barriers that enclose the Middle East play a double role in relation to the region. Like the sturdy walls of a great Middle East Crusader fortress, they are a bulwark of protection, staving off the forays of the outside world and enabling the Middle East communities to pursue their own life. But like fortress walls that have drawbridges and postern gates, the mountains, seas, and deserts also have openings through which the outside world can enter.

Access is possible through four principal gateways that pierce the natural bulwarks. The first is across the narrow strip of sea that separates the Aegean from the Black Sea. Here at the western opening of the passage—the Dardanelles—the fabled heroes of Troy stood their ancient guard. The second gateway is the grassy steppe that lies between the eastern side of the Caspian and the Hindu Kush Mountains of Afghanistan. The third is the Nile Valley, which cuts across the African desert to form a water route (interrupted by cataracts) between the Mediterranean and Central Africa. The fourth is the east-west sea system, the Mediterranean on the west and the Red Sea and Persian Gulf on the east, which extends into the heart of the area.

This combination of protective wall and passable, if widely separated, gates has been a major factor in shaping the history, culture, and destiny of the peoples who live within the Middle East. The protective feature was most effective at the time when it was most needed—as civilization was beginning. Then seas, mountains, and deserts were formidable barriers to invasion, and the people who lived behind the ramparts could develop their societies without being constantly inundated by foreign

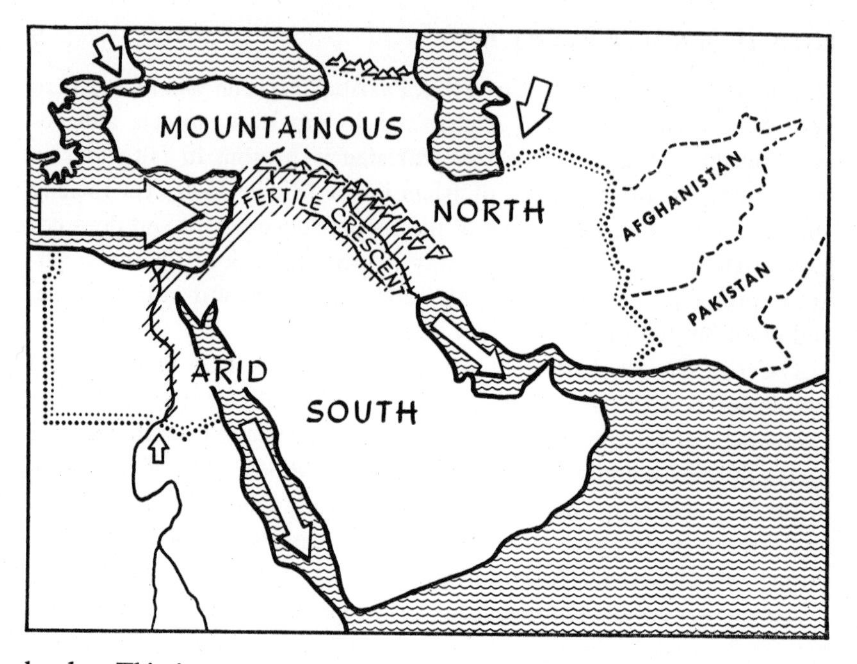

hordes. This is one reason why early civilizations in the Middle East reached such impressive heights. Egypt, Mesopotamia, and Persia all had long centuries of relatively unbroken development that would not have been possible except for the barriers that held back the outside world. One evidence of this is that the Biblical narrative, which covers some three thousand years of history, records no great foreign invasions sweeping across the ancient Middle East. The conflicts and conquerors of its pages all come from within the area itself, with a few exceptions mentioned in vague references that even now are not clearly identified.

Yet the gateways in the protective wall have always been important and often troublesome points of access, opening the life of the otherwise isolated Middle Eastern lands to foreign invasion. Prehistoric man crossed through the western gateway of the Dardanelles and it has remained one of the principal portals for outside influence. Even in the modern world, the use and control of this gateway has been of major importance to the West. One of the causes of the First World War was

Germany's attempt to control Turkey, the possessor of this gateway. Her drive to the East included a plan to build a railroad from Berlin to Baghdad as a permanent hold on this vital route. Indeed, the Dardanelles have been a constant source of international tension in modern times. From 1774 to World War II, no less than fifty-seven treaties and conventions between various European countries dealt with the question of the straits and the problem of control of this gateway to the East.

Because the grassy steppes that lie beyond the Caucasus abut Asia rather than Europe, they have not, in modern times, been the source of as much Western penetration as the Dardanelles. But in the past they played an important role as the corridor through which the mass migrations from central Asia poured into the Middle East. About the second and first milleniums, there came through them the waves of Aryan invasion that contributed the name "Iran" to Persia and brought into the Middle East the important strain of Aryan people. It was through this gateway that the Turkish tribes of the Asiatic heartland came in early medieval days. One group of these, the Ottoman Turks, overran the area and founded an empire that has only expired in modern times. Here, too, was the route of Genghis Khan and his Mongol followers, whose entrance in the thirteenth century was the greatest single catastrophe that ever engulfed the Middle East. Today it is this area that forms the corridor between Russia and India. One reason for the sudden rise of Afghanistan in the consciousness of the Western world is the discovery that once again the Eastern portal of the Middle East may be the key to the control of Asia.

Although the Nile Valley is topographically almost as passable as the Caspian steppes, it has not played as important a role in history. This is due to the fact that the African region beyond has never contained either a great empire or a restless mass of migratory people. During the centuries of ancient Egypt, there was always a trickle of African influence coming down the Nile into the Middle East. For a short period Egypt was ruled by African (Ethiopian) dynasties, among whom was Pharaoh Taharka—that "broken reed" against whom Isaiah warned his countrymen (Isaiah 36:6). Most of the time, though, the influence has been the other way. Because the sources of the Nile lie in the heart of Africa, the rulers of Egypt have always been concerned for the control of the region to the south. Ancient Egypt pushed its conquests as far into the Sudan as possible. And in the modern world, Egypt has claimed a special relation to Sudan because that newly independent country controls all of Egypt's water. Thus, when Gamal Abdel Nasser foresees an African role for Egypt, he is expressing a concern that is inescapable from the view of Egyptian geography.

In the earliest days, the seas that encircle the Middle East were formidable barriers to human movement. Ancient man did not venture far from land in his frail craft, and for many centuries most of the passage to and from the Middle East was by the land routes. How terrifying the sea seemed to the ancient world is shown by the constant use of this word as a symbol of instability and terror throughout the Bible.

With the development of modern navigation, however, the water barrier became a passageway. Because the Mediterranean leads from the heart of Europe to the Middle East, it has become the single most important route of outside influence and interference.

In the sixteenth and seventeenth centuries, England, France, and other European powers established their interests in the area. They not only carried bales of goods to Eastern shores, but planted colonies of merchants whose preferred positions under a special treaty system became offensive to later generations of Middle Eastern nationalists. Even the infant United States was sufficiently concerned for the Mediterranean route to keep a special fleet there under Commodore William Bainbridge. It was the North African corsair threat to our Middle Eastern interests that led the United States into its first foreign war, a story dramatically told in Kenneth Robert's *Lydia Bailey*. Today the Mediterranean is like a great trunk highway, pouring goods, ideas, people, and political interests into the Middle East, linking it inexorably with the life and destiny of the Western world.

The Red Sea with its long finger, the Gulf of Suez, comes to within a hundred miles of the Mediterranean. When the land separating the two seas was penetrated by the Suez Canal in 1869, the most important east-west highway in history was created. Almost overnight Europe's trade with the Orient shifted from the long and uncertain passage around Africa to this safe and short route through the Middle East. But trade is never trade alone; it brings with it privileges, protection, and political interests. An Egyptian stated the situation by saying, "Since the opening of the Suez Canal, the question of whether or not Egypt is to be interfered with by Western powers has been settled; we are going to be interfered with! The question now is—interference by whom and for what purposes?" When President Abdel Nasser of Egypt nationalized the Suez Canal, he recognized this by saying, "Egypt does not own the canal; the canal owns Egypt."

Through this system of gateways, two different influences have entered the Middle East. One is the mass migrations of peoples, principally in ancient times, which flooded the Middle East with divergent racial types. This movement was almost always from north to south. The great center of human restlessness and the hordes it started on the march lay in central Asia, which is the cradle of many of mankind's peoples. Aryans, Scythians, Mongols, Turks all came from beyond the northern ramparts of the Middle East and pressed southward toward its fertile lands and flourishing civilizations. Again and again the prophets of Israel warned that danger to their land and the punishments of God were coming "out of the north." Even today the only serious threat of military invasion comes from across the northern border, where modern Russia looks southward to oil, warm water ports, and international influence.

While the actual migration of people was from north to south, the transient travel of those following world communication has been from west to east. In ancient days it was only a thin trickle of trade that brought spices and silks of the Orient back to the luxury markets of Europe. With the birth of modern commerce, whose manufacturing center is in the Western Hemisphere but whose mass markets are in the East, this west-east movement has become a mighty stream. Tankers, armies, navies, and trading ships of Europe pour eastward across the Mediterranean route. In the Middle East this route divides, one branch going through the Suez Canal to Australia, the Indian Ocean, the East Coast of Africa, and the Far East. The other goes overland from Haifa, Beirut, or Tripoli by truck or rail to the head of the Persian Gulf and thence to the Far East.

It is just because the lands of the Middle East formed the focus of east-west routes that the nations most dependent upon world communications —the expanding imperial powers of the West—gradually sought control of the Middle East. Lord Palmerston, prime minister of Great Britain in the middle of the nineteenth century, reputedly said, "When I travel from London to Birmingham by coach, I expect to have at my disposal a room in a good inn halfway on the road. But I do not intend to own or run the inn myself." This was the theory of Western nations passing through the Middle East; they needed its facilities as a halfway house, but hoped these could be secured without actually taking possession of the region.

The north-south movement of invasion and migration of peoples has made the Middle East racially and culturally diverse. Only occasionally did these migrations create a unified political control, such as the Mongol Empire of Genghis Khan or the longer rule of the Ottoman Turks. As political rule decayed, there were left behind both an intermixture of races and cultures and pockets of the receding racial wave.

The west-east movement of modern world communication has, in contrast, been a unifying force, emphasizing the area concept of the Middle East. It brought Western control in some form to many Eastern lands and created the common resentment against Western pressure that underlies most of the national movements in the Middle East today. The problems posed for Iran by the control of her oil resources by British interests, and the problems of Egypt growing out of the occupation of her Canal Zone by British forces for seventy-four years were not politically the same. But since both arose from the intrusive interests of the outside world and nationalistic reaction to them, they form a bond of sympathy between Egypt and Iran that was absent in ancient times. When Mossadegh, the premier of Iran who nationalized the oil industry, appeared in Cairo he was enthusiastically cheered by Egyptian crowds who saw in him a symbol of their own resistance to "the imperialism of the West."

Yet for all this sympathy, Egypt and Iran have taken opposite sides in their attitude toward the threat of Russia. Iran has aligned itself with the West and is an enthusiastic member of the Baghdad Pact, while Egypt shuns this political, military, and economic alliance and has tried to create a neutralist Arab bloc to oppose it. Thus, when acting from one set of national interests the two countries have very little in common; they do not take a "typical Middle Eastern attitude" toward Russia. But viewed from another set of national interests—the control and development of their own economic resources—they react in a similar pattern.

Here is our basic theme. The Middle East is not so much a geographical area as it is a state of mind; a state of mind that arises principally out of the relation of the region to the outside world. To talk about the Middle East without specifying what problems are under consideration is almost meaningless. Sometimes the lands at the eastern end of the Mediterranean are in the Middle East; sometimes they are as far apart as Tacoma and Timbuktu. To know when the Middle East is really the Middle East is the beginning of wisdom.

2

Mountains, Plains, and Rivers

ASK the nomad or farmer of the Middle East about the lands in which he lives and you receive an answer that goes straight to the point. "We have either the desert or the sown," he will say. "Nothing else."

Unscientific as this description is to the geographer, it is strictly accurate from the standpoint of the man who lives on the geography. To him, rainfall sufficient to grow crops is the chief concern. Where there is water there is life—whether it be in the mountains, river valleys, plains, or desert. Where there is no water, nothing really matters.

A sharp contrast between fertility and barrenness characterizes the entire Middle East, but it is seen at its clearest in the Nile Valley. Here the green fields, watered by the rivers, end abruptly at the foot of the rocky cliff that halts the irrigation canals. It is possible to stand with one foot in rustling wheat fields and the other in arid sands—so close do the "sown" and the desert lie side by side. Some archeologists think that this marked proximity of life and death accounts for the absorption of ancient Egypt in the problems of immortality to which much of its life and wealth were devoted. "In the midst of life we are in death," is the constant warning of the Nile Valley, so green and flourishing in such an ageless sterile waste.

Other areas, like the valleys of the Tigris-Euphrates Rivers, have heavier rainfall and less precise limits of fertility than the Nile Valley, but the fact of the desert is everywhere present in Middle Eastern life and has been for centuries. In the Bible the "wilderness" is always breaking into the narrative (one concordance lists over three hundred versions of this word and its synonyms) and the word "water" often carries a lyric and mystic quality. "Come to the waters," cries Isaiah, and no invitation could fall more appealingly on Eastern ears. Water in the Middle East is always the "water of life."

In more scientific terms, one of the basic factors determining human life and its activities is rainfall. As the acompanying map shows, the precipitation throughout the area is at best scanty. Along the Mediterranean seacoast whose westerly winds are laden with ocean moisture, there is a narrow band of fertility that receives as much as ten or more inches of rainfall a year. This includes the coastal strip of Egypt, Palestine, Lebanon, Syria, and western Turkey. Around the southern end of the Caspian there is also a region of high rainfall. Here water is so abundant that semi-tropical conditions and fruits are found. But once across the mountain ranges that parallel the Mediterranean coast line, the rainfall sharply decreases. Cairo, only 140 miles inland, usually receives less than two inches of rain a year. In many parts of the desert areas rain may fall once or twice in a decade.

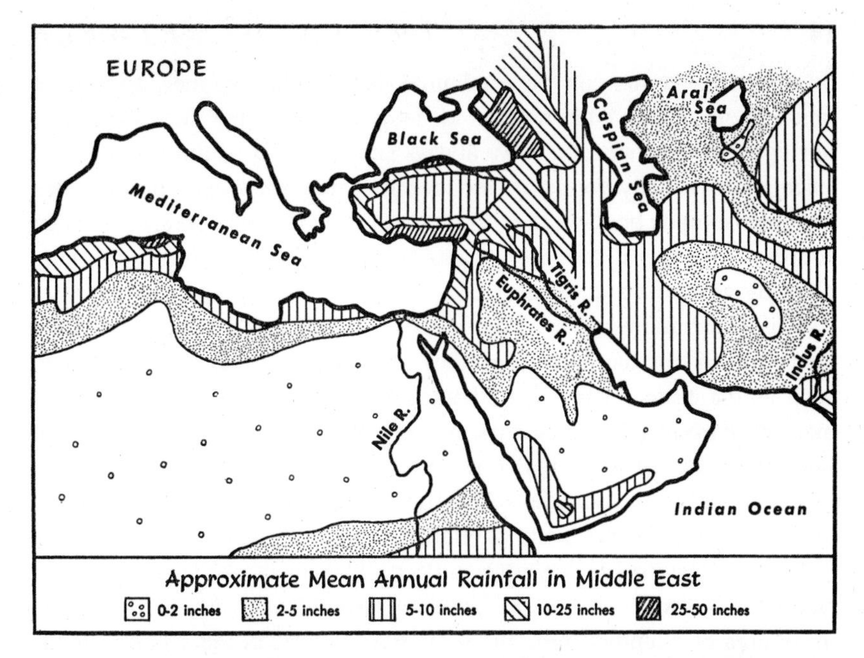

Approximate Mean Annual Rainfall in Middle East

Not only is rainfall scanty, it is also unpredictable. While rainy weather is usually confined to the late fall, winter, and early spring, the amount of rain in these months may vary sharply from year to year. The farmer is never sure that the usual winter rains will really be as usual. What looks like a respectable "annual average" over a decade may, in fact, represent a few heavy deluges followed by seasons of drought.

Because of these conditions only a small part of the Middle East is arable. While exact figures are not available, it is probably true that only between 6 and 8 per cent of the Middle East has sufficient water to be kept under cultivation; the other 92 to 94 per cent is perennially barren. This is almost like saying that out of the entire area of the United States, only California and Oregon can be used for agriculture.

Water is available to the farmer in different forms. In some areas winter rainfall is sufficient to permit crops to be grown without irrigation. Winter rainfall also replenishes the rivers that support intensive irrigation systems in other areas. (The run-off from the winter rains, initially preserved as snow, can be used until late in the summer, forming a much more dependable source of moisture than the rainfall itself.) Springs, ground water fed, have always supported agricultural life. These springs are usually found in mountainous regions where porous rock strata have made possible the formation of such natural and ageless water sources. In a few desert areas oases have grown up around pools supplied by ground water seepage.

The distribution and availablity of water determine not only whether men shall live or die, but where they shall live and die. In fertile areas, such as the eastern part of the United States, the sites of human settlement were frequently selected because of their relation to communications—on the banks of rivers that formed a passage through the forest, or on trails that led to the outside world. But in the Middle East it is not communication that makes a site habitable; it is the available water supply.

Middle Eastern life has always been strongly marked with an oasis character—clusters of families gathered around a spring, a river bank, or an area of abundant rainfall. Some have described this as an "island" culture in which society consists of limited, self-contained settlements set amidst the surrounding aridity. Except for caravan travel, the island dwellers were confined to their own narrow society. Like ships traversing the ocean, the caravans passed over the barren wastes from island to island of human life. This is one reason why the coming of the automobile and the airplane is working such revolutionary changes in Eastern life. For the first time since man appeared in the Middle East, he is able to get out of his island environment easily to mix with other groups.

An important result of this island culture has been its emphasis on the primary role of local loyalties. In ancient times the typical political organization of the Middle East was a small, local state. Each island or island cluster had its own independent political identity. (The Old Testament is filled with a succession of petty kings and kingdoms; each representing an island community that persisted until superior military force overcame it.) Syrians, Egyptians, Babylonians, and Persians imposed their rule on island clusters and for a time forced them into a single state.

But when this state decayed, the old local loyalties reappeared. Even today local loyalties continue as the immediate horizon of much of the Middle East's political consciousness. Egyptian peasants still think of themselves as Saidi (Upper Egyptian) or Bahri (Lower Egyptian), although they have lived under some form of national state since about 3200 B.C. This regional identification began in the dawn of history when the Nile Valley was divided into Upper and Lower Kingdoms.

In addition to the desert and the sown there is another division that runs across the Middle East. This is more strictly a geographical separation, dividing the area into three general regions—north, south, and central.

The chief characteristic of the northern section of the Middle East is its mountain ranges. These start in Turkey as the Taurus Mountains, run eastward into Iran and there divide into the Elburz range in the north and the Zagros in the south, enclosing between them the high barren plateau of central Iran. The mountains are lofty, jagged, and faulted, belonging to the same "young" type as the Alps. The highest peak is Demavend, in the Elburz range, with an altitude of 18,600 feet.

This mountainous northern area has always lived a life largely independent of the rest of the Middle East. Its southern border, lying along the edge of the Mesopotamian valley, forms a natural barrier to racial and linguistic invasion from the south. The Arabs, for instance, moved from the heart of the Arabian Peninsula north and west until they came to the mountain wall. There the faith of the Arabs (Islam) leaped the barrier, but their language and customs did not penetrate to the Persian and Byzantine heartland. Conversely, when Iran and Turkey dominated the Middle East, their political control stretched beyond the mountain ramparts but they were unable to impose their languages and customs permanently on the central and southern portions of the area.

The separate life of the northern section in relation to the rest of the Middle East continues to the present time. When Turkey modernized herself under Mustafa Kemal, she did not turn to the Arab south but to Europe, which lay beyond her northern frontiers. In such typically

Middle Eastern problems as the creation of Israel or control of the Suez Canal, Turkey and Iran have not followed the policies of the Arab states but have adopted independent courses of their own.

At the end of World War II, the Arab countries of the southland organized their own Arab League, which included most of the states south of the mountains. The northern Muslim powers were not invited to join nor did they expect an invitation—so strong is the sense of separate existence. Even the word "Arab" is often a reproach in the northern lands where the Arab came as a conqueror.

The southern region of the Middle East, which includes most of the Arabian Peninsula and Egypt, is largely composed of parched desert and barren wilderness. What elevations there are come mainly from the tilting of entire plateaus. Arabia, for example, is inclined from north to south. Because there are few mountain ranges to make travel difficult, the dry southern area is the home of the nomad who wanders across the desert following the path of the rains. The Beni Shammar, one of the largest of the Arab Bedouin tribes, trek from the heart of Arabia to the gates of Damascus every year in search of pasture. Travel is never easy, of course, for every journey must be made across barren wastes. But the lack of forbidding mountain passes, blocked by heavy winter snows, permits the nomad to travel when and where he pleases—as long as he has stamina and knows the water holes.

Out of the barren southland have come many ancient invasions. The Arameans, the Hebrew tribes, and the Muslim Arabs, all driven by the barrenness of their homeland, wandered northward into the fertile river valleys of the central section. Their advance was stopped only when they were confronted by the mountain ranges. Their blood and culture permanently mixed with the central sections they conquered. Today the common speech of the Middle East south of the mountain barriers is the desert language of Arabic. This heritage was brought by the invading Arabs in their religious conquests of the seventh and eighth centuries.

Lying between the mountainous north and the desert south is the central portion of the Middle East, the Fertile Crescent. This area is neither mainly mountainous nor mainly desert but a mixture of the two. Mountains especially characterize the western end, where the Lebanon and anti-Lebanon ranges, running from north to south, finally melt away into the Judean hills. Arms of the southern desert reach into the Fertile Crescent, stretching particularly into Syria and Jordan. But the heart of the central region is a system of rivers that creates a belt of fertility and a travel route between the Persian Gulf and the Mediterranean.

The eastern half of the Fertile Crescent is dominated by the Tigris and the Euphrates, the twin rivers of Iraq (ancient Mesopotamia). Rising in the mountains of eastern Turkey, they flow south and east and enfold between them some of the richest fields of the Middle East. At the western end of the Fertile Crescent, in Syria and Lebanon, there are a series of short rivers born in the snows of the mountain ranges. These make the valley that lies between the two Lebanon ranges a paradise of wheat fields and fruit groves.

As the Fertile Crescent turns south to enter Palestine it becomes narrower. Here the desert comes up to the east bank of the Jordan and invades the southern part of Palestine, finally reaching to the sea in the stark Sinai Peninsula. A few days' journey over a waste of sand dunes and jagged hills reveals the Nile Valley, whose lush fields mark the end of continuous fertility. West of Egypt there are rain-watered coastal areas that in times past supported flourishing rural communities. These are so separated by desert stretches, however, that they can be considered to form a series of isolated oases rather than an extension of the Fertile Crescent.

The Fertile Crescent plays a double role in the life of the Middle East. Because its river systems provide an abundant and unfailing source of water, it has been the granary of the area. Here primitive man first learned the skills of irrigation. In learning, he laid the basis of civilization whose prerequisite is that men shall work together in communities—as they must to control and harness a river. Here, too, many of our common cereals—wheat, barley, oats—were first domesticated, and they have been cultivated in rustling fields since the earliest records of history.

It was partly to Egypt and Syria that Rome turned for the cereal that fed her multitudes, and today grain is still a principal export of Iraq and Syria.

It is natural that the people who live in the barren lands on either side have always sought to invade and possess this granary. Protected on the north by mountain ranges, the southern edge of the Fertile Crescent fades into the desert wastes without any natural barriers except a sea of sand. But aridity and sand are no barriers to wandering nomad tribes. Repeatedly the dwellers in the Arabian Peninsula have pushed northward toward the Tigris-Euphrates Valley whenever their strength, or their foe's weakness, permitted. The Hebrew tribes were one of these wandering desert groups who pressed out of their wilderness home to possess a land "flowing with milk and honey."

At times these invasions came as organized military conquests. More frequently they have been the lightning raids of Arab tribesmen who swept in for a brief hour of plunder and then disappeared back into the vastness of their desert. Sometimes these raids were sufficiently large and repeated to result in the permanent infiltration of nomads. These settled on the land and were gradually transformed into farmers. One such group is the Muntafiq confederation of tribes. A nomadic group some two centuries ago, they are now farming on the banks of the Euphrates.

But the Fertile Crescent is not only a granary to be conquered; it is also a natural path of communication from east to west. Someone has described it as the spinal column of the Middle East that carries the major impulses of the entire area. Whether it was the caravan trails of ancient times, the Berlin-to-Baghdad railway of German dreams, or the streams of trucks traveling over modern highways, it was only through the Fertile Crescent that an easy route was possible. Not until the advent of flight could one travel from historic centers like Cairo, Damascus, and Tehran without regard to this natural highway.

It was under the favorable conditions of the Fertile Crescent that the earliest empires developed. Egypt began at the western end and Assyria, Babylonia, and Persia at the eastern. Because these powers were often in contact with one another across the Fertile Crescent highway, they were engaged in continuing conflict to control its whole length. Ancient Egyptian forces penetrated into the upper Euphrates Valley and for a time dominated the life of the petty kingdoms there. Later the armies of Sennacherib the Assyrian and Cyrus the Persian traveled westward over the Crescent route to war with Egypt for the control of the Mediterranean seacoast. It was in the course of these invasions that the Hebrew kingdoms of Judah and Israel were wiped out. Centuries later Rome tried to control the entire Fertile Crescent area only to be stopped by the fierce power of the Parthian, who had extended an aggressive empire westward along the old invasion routes from northern Iran.

Because of the functional importance of the Fertile Crescent, the Arab countries that possess or border it are sensitive to any intrusion. To let any part of the Fertile Crescent fall into foreign hands is to cut off the countries at either end from contact with one another. This is especially true in Palestine, where the desert comes within a few miles of the seacoast and the main route of travel runs between the river Jordan and the sea. When this area is in foreign hands, Egypt and her northern Arab neighbors are separated. For this reason, Egypt has frequently sought to control Palestine. Many centuries before the ancient Hebrew kingdoms, the land as far north as Damascus was an Egyptian "area of influence." Under the Muslim champion Saladin, Palestine was again controlled from Egypt. And during the nineteenth century, Egypt under the armies of Muhammad Ali reasserted a short sway.

Because of Palestine's position athwart the Fertile Crescent highway, its neighboring states have only acquiesced in its independent existence during the periods when they were too divided or too weak to conquer it, or when Palestine itself was supported by some dominant outside power. The original conquest of the Holy Land by the Crusaders was possible because it occurred at a moment when dynastic feuds were weakening the caliphate. But as soon as a leader arose to unite the Arab world, the Christian kingdom of Jerusalem faced a pressure to which it finally had to yield. When Christian Europe could supply arms and money, Christian

Palestine existed; when these were gone, the surrounding Arab states reclaimed the land as part of the Fertile Crescent.

The geographical factor is one reason why the creation of modern Israel has raised such a storm in the Arab world. With Palestine in the possession of and supported by a non-Arab power, Egypt and Muslim North Africa are barred from their natural contacts with the rest of the Arab world. Today the Arabs react to Israel just as they reacted to the Crusaders. And it is interesting to note that President Nasser of Egypt is hailed in Arab lands as the "second Saladin." As in the case of the Crusader kingdoms, the establishment of Israel was only possible because it was supported by Western funds and leadership. Whether the new state can become permanently established and accepted by the Arab Middle East when Western support and financing is withdrawn remains to be seen. History does not always repeat itself, but at least its lessons should be read with a perceptive eye and an inquiring mind.

This brief survey of rainfall and topography does not exhaust the regional differences within the boundaries of the Middle East. There are many small areas that have sharply marked geographical characteristics, giving each a distinctive life of its own. On the lower reaches of the Tigris and Euphrates in southern Iraq is a great swamp where the marsh Arabs live the life of a primitive Venice. Hidden by tall reeds, their mat-built villages are perched on low mounds in the midst of a watery waste whose currents make their roadways. Another river region, the Egyptian Delta, is one of the most densely populated agricultural areas in the world. The alluvial soil in the region is so rich and the water so plentiful that three or four crops a year can be planted. Anyone traveling by train from Luxor on the Upper Nile to Alexandria notes that after Cairo the villages rush past the window in almost continuous procession, and the landscape is verdant with perennial green as far as the eye can see.

A unique region is located at the southern end of the Arabian Peninsula. Here the monsoon rains of the Indian Ocean make the highlands redolent with frankincense. It was this green and fragrant land that beguiled the Romans into naming the entire area Arabia Felix—Fertile

Arabia—to the bewilderment of all travelers who toil across the burning sands of the Arabian desert. And far to the west on the North African coast lies another agricultural region whose vineyards and wheat fields are a major economic asset to France.

The Caspian Plains, mentioned earlier, also are noteworthy. Their rich, almost sub-tropical fertility seems strangely out of place in an area composed chiefly of wilderness and barren mountains.

Desert and sown; mountains, plains, and rivers; these all are a reminder of our opening observation that there is really no Middle-East-in-itself. Were it not for the surrounding continents that force such marked divergencies to live side by side, it is doubtful if a Middle East would exist at all. Varieties of physical environment produce varieties of human society. The problems of existing in the desert are radically different from those of supporting life on the banks of the Euphrates, and the roving nomad is therefore different from the agricultural peasant. Political power may shift and the tides of conquest ebb and flow, but the geography does not change. The lack of rain, the northern mountain barrier, the Fertile Crescent, and the oases-limited horizons of life are still basic and inescapable factors in deciding the destiny and determining the reactions of the people who live in the varied Middle East.

3

The Sons of Adam

ℭ ONLY in America, it is said, can a true "European" be found, for here the parent stocks of the Old World have blended in the melting pot of the New to produce a continental man. Europe itself has only Swedes, Poles, Magyars, Italians, Irish, English, to mention a few of the diverse nationalities that live within its borders.

But there is no "new world" in which the diverse groups of the Middle East have mixed to produce a single or typical Middle Eastern man. There are Arabs, Turks, Egyptians, Persians, Kurds—all amalgams of ancient peoples but distinct, one from the other. As in topography and climate, so the "sons of Adams" (as the Arab calls the human race) show such marked differences that it is impossible to include them in a single category. Indeed, few other areas of the world display as wide a range of racial variation as the lands at the eastern end of the Mediterranean. Here is a medley of nationalities that not only changes from country to country, but also from one population island to another.

For milleniums mass migrations have pressed across the continental frontiers, bringing new blood into the Middle East. Some of these invasions brought permanent settlers, and new racial types resulted as the conqueror's blood mingled with the conquered. Some migrations ebbed away almost as quickly as they came, leaving behind racial pockets that have preserved their own identity until the present time. The earliest of these invasions lies in the dawn of history. Then Mediterranean men overran the area and contributed to it the foundation stock on which many later racial invasions were grafted. Among the latest is the movement of European Jews to Israel, which not only is introducing a European racial strain into the Middle East, but is coalescing with the Oriental Jew to produce what will probably become a new Middle Eastern race—the Israeli.

There is still no completely scientific method of classifying the families of man. The old theory of "races" (brown, yellow, red, black, white) has been abandoned because color is not a universally determining factor in human groupings. Language, on the other hand, is merely a cultural classification. Among the Arabic speaking peoples, for example, are found such different types as the peasant of the Nile Valley—with his kinship to the ancient Egyptians—and the spare, hawk-nosed nomad of the desert Bedouin tribes. Nor does nationality accurately classify people, for not only are there parts of the Middle East where this concept is scarcely known, but within any one nation (such as Iran) there are multiple groups (Persian, Turk, Arab) with obvious physical differences. Head measurements (the relation of width to length) furnish a more dependable method of classification, but tell the layman little about the distinctive characteristics in which he is interested. Only when all these factors are considered together does a picture of the sons of Adam emerge.

While the racial types in the Middle East vary from region to region, the basic elements in the different mixtures can be identified. The oldest and most important is Mediterranean man. In prehistoric times this group was widely distributed around the Mediterranean sea basin, including parts of Western Europe (where the Cornish, Welsh, Irish, and Bretons represent the strain today) and in India, whose original stock showed strong Mediterranean affinity. Mediterranean man was long headed, of moderate build, with brown and wavy hair. In early times he was the principal inhabitant of the Middle East and it was in amalgamation with him that most later racial types developed.

The second racial element is the Armenoid group, a branch of the great Alpine race that ran east to west across Eurasia. As seen in many Armenians, Armenoid characteristics are a round head with a flattened back, dark hair and eyes, and a prominent, strongly curved nose. This latter is popularly considered a distinctly "Semitic," especially Jewish, feature. But it is found among Arab tribesmen and also in non-Semitic Iran, where the phrase "may your nose always be fat" is a polite expression of personal praise. Actually, the "Semitic" nose is a contribution of the Armenoid group to many different races in the Middle East. Like Mediterranean man, the Armenoids entered the Middle East early in its history, possibly coming out of Central Asia.

A possible relative of the Armenoid is the Iranian group, usually classified as another branch of the Alpine race. The head is less round than in the Armenoid and the color of hair and eyes lighter. Although this group is chiefly found today in the country of Iran, as an element in racial mixtures it can be traced westward to the coast of the Mediterranean and even to the islands of Cyprus and Crete.

A fourth parent stock is a branch of the Aryan race, called by some anthropologists Proto-Nordic. As the name suggests, this group shares the characteristics of the north European Nordic people—long heads with tall stature and fair hair. The Proto-Nords entered the Middle East in historic times as part of a mass movement that took the Aryan race eastward into India, westward into Greece, and northward into Europe.

Another group is the Turki. Coming from their homeland in central Asia, the Turki peoples frequently show such marked Mongolian features as a slight yellowness of the skin, round heads, black straight hair, and "almond" eyes. Politically, the Turkis have played an important role in the Middle East. Modern representatives are the Ottoman Turks who rose to power in the fourteenth and fifteenth centuries and established the great Turkish Empire. Genghis Khan and his followers also belonged to this group and their influx into the Middle East left behind small pockets of Mongol identity.

Out of the mixture of these and many lesser groups have come the varying racial characteristics that form the ethnic picture of the Middle East today. Arabia, the homeland of the Arab, shows strong Mediterranean man characteristics. This means that the typical desert Arab is best considered as a fairly pure representative of Mediterranean man, despite the characteristic "Semitic" nose. Areas of lesser racial mixture lie north and south of the Fertile Crescent, in the mountains of Iran and the deserts of Arabia. This reflects the transit role of the Fertile Crescent along whose river valleys invaders traveled east and west and finally settled to amalgamate with the conquered peoples.

If detailed racial classification of Middle Easterners is difficult, linguistic grouping is easier, and perhaps more illuminating. Language and culture seem to differentiate people much more than do round heads and hooked noses.

The languages of the Middle East fall into three major groups, each defined by its vocabulary and grammatical structure and its relation to the great families of languages. The most widespread is the Semitic, of which Arabic is the chief contemporary representative. The Semitic languages have practically nothing in common with the Indo-European tongues familiar in the Western world. They represent a different type of language structure, based upon a verb composed of consonants with vowels playing such a secondary role that often they are unwritten.

Semitic language groups have been a major constituent of the Middle East since antiquity. The earliest recorded Semitic language was Akkadian, the tongue of the upper Mesopotamian Valley in the twenty-third century B.C. It was written in cuneiform characters (adopted from the conquered non-Semitic Sumerians) and was the parent both of Assyrian (northern Mesopotamia) and Babylonian (southern Mesopotamia). A later development of the Semitic group was Aramaic, which for many centuries was the language of commerce and diplomacy in regions as far apart as Persia and Egypt. The rise of Aramaic is reflected in the later part of the Old Testament, where Aramaic words occur in the books of Job, the later Psalms, Jonah, and Esther. By New Testament times, Aramaic had supplanted Hebrew as the popular speech of Palestine and it undoubtedly was the language Jesus spoke. Today this ancient tongue is preserved as the language of liturgy in a few older churches and is said still to be spoken in one or two villages near Damascus.

Other ancient Semitic tongues were Syriac, an Aramaic dialect in which one of the earliest translations of the Bible was made; Phoenician, which gave the world its basic phonetic alphabet; Punic, a Phoenician dialect and the language of Carthage in North Africa (believed to be preserved in some Maltese words); and Hebrew, long virtually a dead language but being reborn in Israel today.

But of all the Semitic tongues, it is Arabic that has spread the farthest and is used by the greatest number of people. Coming out of the heart of Arabia with the Muslim conquerors, it has become the sacred language of Islam and the ordinary speech of most of the area lying south of the northern mountain tier. Even beyond this barrier, where Turkish and Persian remained the national languages, the Arabic script and many Arabic words were adopted. "Wisdom" say the Arabs, "descended from Allah on the hand of the Frank and the tongue of the Arab" and certainly the "tongue of the Arab" is one of the strongest unifying factors in the middle East.

Yet Arabic itself has sharp regional differences. The classical, written language is virtually the same everywhere—like the Latin of medieval

Europe. It forms a bond of communication that can be understood by at least one person in every community from Morocco on the west to Aden on the east. But the spoken language varies from country to country; so much so that the local dialect of a North African Arab is almost incomprehensible to the nomad of Arabia. Accent and pronunciation differ, vocabulary has been altered, and grammatical changes have been adopted that almost make the local tongues true national languages.

Thus when we speak of the "Semites" or even of the "Arabs" we are not speaking of a racial group, but of people who speak one of the languages enumerated above. Egyptians, for instance, often spoke Coptic until about the fourteenth century, when the Arabic tongue of their Muslim conquerors became the common speech of the countryside. No one would maintain that Egyptians suddenly altered because they began to use Arabic, yet today they can be classed as Arabs in the only sense in which that word has clearly defined meaning—a speaker of Arabic.

The second linguistic group is composed of Indo-European languages. As the name indicates, these originated outside the Middle East and belong to that family of tongues spoken today in most of the Western hemisphere. Because the Indo-European languages came with a tide of immigration and conquest across the northern borders of the Middle East, they are found most commonly and widely in the northern tier, whose mountain ramparts have already been shown to be a barrier to movement southward.

In ancient times, there were several Indo-European languages in the Middle East. Avestan, the tongue of the Persian Empire of Darius, was such a language, as also was Hittite, the speech of that strange people of Anatolia who overran the western part of the Middle East in the second millenium. Ancient Greek must also be classified as a Middle Eastern Indo-European language, not only because there were extensive Greek colonies in what is now Turkey (Ionia) but because Koine, literary Greek, was a major language of communication in the late Greek and Roman period. The great book of the Middle East, the New Testament, was written in Koine Greek. Modern Persian is the most important representative of the Indo-European languages in the Middle East today.

Like the Indo-European languages, the third group of tongues found in the Middle East had a foreign origin and came across the northern border with invading tribes. From central Asia came invaders who brought with them various dialects of the Turanian group. The Ottoman Turks brought such a language, and their tongue became the Turkish speech that a century ago was the language of state throughout the Arab world and North Africa. Today it is confined almost entirely to the modern state of Turkey. Because the Turks were untutored nomads at the beginning of their power, their language was strongly affected by the territories they overran—Persia and the Arab world. The Turks adopted the Arabic alphabet and many Arabic and Persian words, as well as the literary forms of these languages. But when Mustafa Kemal turned Turkey toward the West, repudiating its historic Islamic and Arab connections, he discarded the Arabic alphabet in favor of Latin characters, and sought to purge the Turkish language of its dependence upon an Arabic vocabulary. By thus cutting Turkish from its Arabic past, he gave a new generation a fresh start toward the future. Today a new literature with a new script and new words has arisen in Turkey. But the price paid for this innovation is that the great classics of the past are closed to the modern Turk.

Turkish belongs to the same family of languages as Finnish and Magyar, which also came with invading groups out of central Asia. Other Turanian languages in the Middle East are found in Iran and Afghanistan.

While speech is a sharp and ever present classifier of the sons of Adam, there is another factor that runs across racial and religious lines to create certain broad divisions within Middle Eastern life. This is the type of social organization in which people live. Such organizations are shaped partly by the effect of environment on human activity, and partly by custom and tradition. Common patterns of life, shared by people whose nationality, speech, and race may differ, form one of the bonds that helps create the Middle East—this bond of shared experience makes the farmer in Iran understand and feel akin to the fellah in Egypt.

In many Western eyes, the most familiar figure of the Middle East is the roaming tribesman of the desert, swathed in robes against the scorching sun and traveling by caravan across the sandy wastes. Familiar he certainly is, for the Middle East is the home of the nomad whose restless itinerant life exercises a special fascination to the house-bound people of the Western world. Yet the nomad is only a fraction of the Middle Eastern population, and to judge the entire area through the tradition that makes him its typical figure is to misunderstand the scene.

Nomadism is the result of environment and man's struggle to keep alive within it. In areas where rainfall is scanty, it is easier to follow the rains across the desert than to settle in one spot and wrestle with perennial drought. Lacking the requisites of permanent agriculture, man becomes a raiser of flocks and herds whose needs set the pattern of his life.

This method of supporting life necessarily produces a distinctive society. Nomadic society is a society that never settles down on one spot of land but lives by roving. Individual land ownership has little meaning. Tribal rights to grazing and watering places for sheep and camels are a necessity; they are, as well, a cause for fierce dispute and rivalry. Recently an entire Point Four project in Iran had to be redesigned because its consummation would have made the Bakhtiari tribe travel on the wrong side of a mountain pass during its annual migration. This would have infringed on the traditional area of another tribal group, thus laying the Bakhtiari open to vendettas from the "wronged" tribe. It was such disputed grazing grounds that made Abraham and Lot go their separate ways lest there be "strife between your herdsmen and my herdsmen; for we are kinsmen."

The nomad's loyalty is to his own family and tribe and not to some distant central government. This narrow loyalty was the problem that confronted Abdul Azziz Ibn Saud when he tried to bring the nomadic tribes of the desert together to form the Saudi Kingdom. It was also the problem of Muhammad, thirteen centuries earlier, when he established the new community of Islam within the strong tribal society of seventh century Arabia. Both attempts took a skillful combination of force and diplomacy. If a tribe could not be defeated, it might be brought into the larger group through blood relationship. This is one reason why both Muhammad and Abdul Azziz were prolific in their marriages.

Along with his tribal loyalty, the nomad is an unabating individualist. He has no landlord to control him, no government to tax him, no parliament to decide his destiny. The community in which he lives is led by its sheikh, but the sheikh is only accepted by the tribe as long as he shows the ability to master the problems of tribal life. When he fails someone else takes his place—usually from the chieftain's family but not necessarily a son or brother. This gives nomadic life a certain rough democracy and equalitarian spirit.

The single largest area of nomadism is the interior of the Arabian Peninsula, where large tribes still keep to the ancient pattern of their wandering life. Nomad groups are also found in Egypt, Jordan, Iraq, Syria, and North Africa. There are also several nomadic tribes in Iran, of which the Bakhtiari and the Kashghai are the most noted.

The nomad plays a triple role in Middle Eastern life. He is a raiser of cattle as well as of sheep and camels. In fact, one of the problems in settling the nomad as an agriculturist is that he tends to give up raising these animals with a consequent economic loss to the country.

The nomad is also a political problem. Strongly individualistic, he does not take kindly to the ways of centralized government. Taxes, military service, and criminal law procedures seem to him to curtail his freedom. The Biblical story of the dreadful oppression of the children of Israel through forced labor in Egypt has a remarkably nomadic ring to it. In the same way, modern Arab tribes of Egypt's Sinai Peninsula resent the government's labor draft required for road building and irrigation—all plain necessities to the farmer, but petty tyranny to the Bedouin who travels his own desert trail and seldom grows anything.

Moreover, the nomad inevitably clashes with the settled population of agricultural districts. As improvements in irrigation make it possible to farm hitherto arid land, tribal pastures dwindle. The resulting friction between nomad and farmer makes the nomad a constant threat to civil authority. This is one of the problems that has long beset Iran, where the great nomadic tribes are sometimes in arms against the national government for what they believe to be a violation of their historic rights.

Nomadism is of particular interest to the Christian because of its influence in shaping the basic character of Semitic religion. The concept of a "chosen" people who are in some special sense the "tribe of God" is a reflection of the nomadic way of life. The ideal age of the patriarchs when God was the God of "Abraham, Isaac, and Jacob" was a nomadic age. And when the Hebrew tribes, themselves nomads for a generation in Sinai, entered Palestine and settled down into agricultural and later commercial life, the new land-and-money society became a challenge to ideals of equality and property that were inherited from nomad days.

Equally, the life of the nomad has stamped its mark on the great nomadic religion, Islam. Born in the heart of a nomad society, original Islamic ideas reflect the social customs of tribal Arabia. Islam's concept of God, some scholars maintain, is that of the paramount sheikh—powerful, just, gracious to his own tribesmen, yet with a streak of unpredictability. This absence of obedience to a superior moral law differentiates Islam's concepts sharply from the Christian vision. The relation of communities within Islam, both of believers to one another and to the minority groups, also shows a pattern of nomadic tribal life. Just as the fugitive is granted protection in the tents of a rival tribe to which he flees, yet never becomes a full tribal member, so the Christian and Jewish minorities are granted rights of protection and the exercise of their own religious worship, yet are never quite accepted as full members of Islamic society. As the nomadic Age of the Patriarchs stamped its seal on Hebrew religion, so the seventh century life of the Arabian desert has marked Islam indelibly.

Important as the nomads are, however, they are not the largest group in the Middle East, nor is their way of life the most common. By the side of the nomad stands the farmer, representing some 75 per cent of the area's inhabitants. Typically he is called a fellah, or plowman, thus differentiating him from the wandering herdsman who does little agricultural work beyond planting a few moist desert gullies with grain.

At almost every point the farmer differs from the nomad. He spends his life—sometimes his family spends generations—on the same spot. The land, its fertility, availability, and use, determines his life. Because arable land is sharply limited by the scanty rainfall it is the form of wealth most desired. This has made a landlord society as inevitable in the Middle East as a capitalist manufacturing society was in nineteenth century Europe. Indeed, much of the fertile land is owned by large landlords for whom the farmer is a tenant, dependent upon the good will and influence of the owner of his fields for his very life.

The farming population is more politically stable and easily controlled than the nomadic tribesmen. Rarely have there been agricultural revolts in the Middle East. When they have occurred, it is usually because overtaxation or famine has made life unbearable. Even today, when nationalism has become almost a religion, there have been few spontaneous farmers' organizations in the Middle East. Where such parties do exist, they usually result from the efforts of some leader of the upper classes, seeking to organize farmer discontent for his own purposes.

The average Middle Eastern farmer lives in a village surrounded by fields. This arrangement is due to the need for protection, as it was in medieval Europe. There is, then, no clear distinction between the "villager" and the "farmer," for one is simply the other in his home setting. Even large villages of several hundred houses do not differ basically from tiny hamlets. Both are conglomerates of farm families, living together by custom and for protection rather than because of trade—as is often the case in the West.

The farmer, who is bound to his fields and lives on the merest margin of subsistence, is understandably wary of new practices. When pasturage fails or the water holes dry up, the nomad can always move on to fresh fields, but the fellah must exist or perish on his few acres of land. A farmer in America can afford to experiment with a new crop on a few acres of land, knowing that failure will not seriously imperil his standard of living. But the Eastern peasant lives on such a narrow margin that if even a small plot fails to produce as expected, he and his family may starve. Thus when a new practice is suggested to a fellah he will not try it, for he dare not take the risk. This basic fact must be thoroughly understood by those who are trying to better the peasant's life through improving his farming methods. Merely to tell him, or even show him a new agricultural practice is never sufficient. He must see the result for himself, perhaps for as long as five years, before he is sufficiently convinced to risk his family's life on the change. "As stubborn as a fellah," is the Eastern equivalent for "as stubborn as a donkey." Many an educated Arab will say, "You can teach a donkey—but not a fellah." But this is an unjust characterization, for the fellah's stubbornness is born out of bitter experience.

Yet just because the farmer is chained to his land and stubborn in his ways, he forms one of the most basic elements of stability in the Middle East. Governments may change, dynasties be overthrown, foreign conquerors possess the land, but the peasant goes his way with little regard for what happens in the circles of the great. Seed time and harvest are his concern, and until these are disturbed by overwhelming natural catastrophe or unbearable tyranny, he asks only to "be given his irrigation water and left alone." For this reason the political tumult that so often fills Middle Eastern cities with rioting is not so serious a threat to national stability as it would be in the West.

The city dweller stands in marked contrast to the nomad and the farmer. The difference does not arise from race or caste, which do not exist in Muslim lands, but in function and environment. The Middle Eastern city, like a city anywhere else, is a production and trade center. Its citizens live in an atmosphere of political and commercial activity that is far removed from the agricultural horizons of the farming village or town.

City life is shaped by four influences. The first influence is that of trade, which brings with it an interest in the outside world and the flow of ideas that accompanies merchandise from faraway places. For all their exuberant fancy, the pages of the *Arabian Nights* ring true in their picture of merchants on far journeys meeting in the bazaars of Damascus or Baghdad to spend an evening telling tall tales of the world beyond the city's walls. Just so do the patrons of the coffee houses of Cairo discuss the American cotton market, the effect of a drop in the pound sterling, or the latest Russian commercial loan to Afghanistan.

The second urban influence arises from production. While most villages have a few semi-skilled craftsmen, it is in the cities that the manufacture of local goods takes place. Much of this, of course, is still done by hand and there are long bazaar streets devoted to the production of a single type of goods. The craftsman lives by his skill and the fluctuations of the local market, and is keenly aware of all the factors that unsettle his trade or raise the cost of his products. In contrast, the fellah always has his fields to support him, and is indifferent to a world beyond his village.

A third influence comes from the communication resources found in the cities. News travels not only by bazaar rumors, but through books and pamphlets that are cried on the street corners. In modern times newspapers have become widespread. Even those who do not read can sit in a coffee house and hear a more favored friend recite the latest news dispatch on the Eisenhower doctrine, events at a recent meeting of the Baghdad Pact nations, the union of Syria and Egypt, or the counter-union of Jordan and Iraq. Indeed, little goes on anywhere in the world that fails to find its way into the Middle East press. And the radio brings to homes and bazaar shops a roundup of the daily news.

Finally the city is the center of education. In medieval times the famous mosque schools brought students flocking from the countryside. Today the modern university or state secondary school likewise draws its strength from country students who come to the cities for their learning. Not only does this lead to a general diffusion of knowledge, but the frequently violent political restlessness of student groups keeps even the quiet craftsman aware of the currents of new life in his country.

In wealthy circles there is an amalgamation of Eastern and Western culture that makes the cultivated Middle Easterner a stimulating companion. He often knows more about international affairs than his American counterpart and has an appreciation of varied cultures that many Westerners never attain. Even the bazaar merchant, taxi driver, or coppersmith has his opinions about national and international affairs that would be quite incomprehensible to the village farmer. Above all, the city-dweller is living at the spot where the traditional isolation of the Middle East lies open to the influences of the contemporary world. In response to this environment he has developed a wide range of economic and political interests that differentiate him from the bulk of the farming population.

The city is the frontier between the centuries, where the untroubled past of the countryside meets the turbulent currents of modernity. Within recent years almost all Middle Eastern cities have grown alarmingly. The influx of village folk seeking employment or education has only added to the conflict between the old world of settled Islamic practices and the strange forces of modern life. This is one reason why the great cities of the Middle East are centers of political discontent. Here are the riots in protest against the creation of Israel or against the Baghdad Pact; here contending political parties organize student mobs to shout their slogans in the streets—possibly even forcing a government to resign under the pressures of popular hysteria.

Perhaps the Arab is right when he finds no term for this medley of races, languages, and social organizations that form his world except "the sons of Adam." In the end, the Middle Easterner is like man every place else—a human individual whose customs and attitudes are set by the influences that play upon him. And because these influences are as diverse as geography, history, and social factors can make them, the people who live in the Middle East must be considered against their own particular backgrounds and not under some inclusive term that stamps them uniformly as "Middle Eastern" men and women.

4

The Bonds of Culture and Faith

"WHAT I like about the Middle East," said an American tourist, "is that you can pick your century." Anyone who has traveled through these Eastern lands knows at once what he meant. Standing under the full moon at Cheops' pyramid, the centuries dissolve and with Moses one surveys the "riches of Egypt" in the days of the pharaohs. Or wander through the bazaars of Baghdad, and the Arabian Nights become plausibly contemporary. Yet in the palatial Hilton Hotel at Istanbul or the Misr Spinning Works in the Nile Delta, the twentieth century is as present and impressive as in any city of the West.

This intermingling of the centuries is not simply a matter of archeology and ancient buildings. It is a vivid facet of the culture and customs of the contemporary Middle East. In the heart of the Cairo bazaars, apprentice lads learn their craft in copper, silver, and leather under the same system that flourished in the days of the Mamelukes (thirteenth to sixteenth centuries). Yet across the Nile stands an Egyptian university, training doctors, engineers, and scientists with thoroughly modern methods and curricula. In 1947, the Egyptian Department of Health used modern epidemic control techniques to halt an outbreak of cholera, while on the streets of Cairo hawkers sold charms whose magic spell had been invoked since the days of the ancient papyrii. Indeed you can pick your century in the Middle East!

But the centuries stand separated by a great divide—A.D. 622. In June of that year, Muhammad, the caravan leader of Mecca whose religious convictions gave birth to the Muslim faith, shook the dust of his dissenting home city from his garments and hastened to the neighboring town of Medina. There he established the first fully Muslim community. The *hijrah,* the Muslim calls his journey, the "flight." By this flight all history is divided into the "days of ignorance" before Islam and "days of enlightenment" after its coming. That is why the Muslim calendar is dated "A.H."—"after the *hijrah.*" Nineteen hundred fifty-eight, Anno Domini, is 1377 after the *hijrah,* and while the Muslim merchant may use the Western date for his business, it is his sense of living A.H. that furnishes his view of history and its events.

Primarily that view is based upon the emergence of Islam as the triumphant faith of the Middle East. Christians see in their religion's rapid conquest of the Roman Empire a mark of its truth and power, but Islam marched across the world more swiftly than Christianity. Within a century after Muhammad's death, his followers controlled the greatest empire the world had seen—embracing Spain on the west, the coast of North Africa, and the entire Middle East as we have defined it with the exception of what is now Turkey. Of course the majority of people living within these borders were not yet Muslims. However, the privileged position of the Muslim, the pressure of social prestige, the weight of discriminatory taxation, as well as genuine conversion gradually won the conquered peoples to the new religion.

For the first time in history, the natural diversities of Middle Eastern lands were overlaid by an almost universal faith. It is true that Christianity before the rise of Islam was a dominant faith in the western part of the region. But it was divided by sectarian differences, and oppression in some areas made Christian groups there actually welcome the Muslim conqueror. In the eastern part of the Middle East, Christians formed minority communities. The Sassanian Empire of Persia was Zoroastrian and the tribes of Arabia were chiefly pagan.

Islam itself did not escape from sectarianism and it was not long before Muslims were raising the sword against their brothers in the faith. Yet, for all its divisions, Islam furnished a new experience of religious brotherhood that created a community of feeling from one end of the Muslim world to the other. Originally Islam consciously set itself in opposition to the tribal and nationalistic loyalties of its day and its followers thought of themselves first as Muslims and only second as Arabs, Persians, or Egyptians. Such a dominant religious community inevitably excluded the members of different faiths. The other monotheists (principally Jews, Christians, and Sabeans) were given the right to continue their worship and enjoy community security, but they were forever separated from the brotherhood of the faithful. Today, these groups that accommodated themselves to their Muslim environment through the centuries retain a sharp sense of religious difference that often cloaks a basic fear of the majority.

After the *hijrah,* A.H., marks more than the beginning of a new religion in the Middle East; it is also the beginning of a new cultural achievement. Like most cultural developments, the raw materials were drawn from the older civilizations that were overrun and absorbed. The richness of the Islamic culture, one scholar has said, is due to two factors—a hunger for ideas, and older civilizations on which to feed. Out of these developed the world of thought, faith, and social practice in which so much of the Middle East lives. This world is shared by everyone who calls himself "Muslim," be he Iranian, Turk, or Arab. Even the non-Muslim minorities are affected by the "Muslimness" of the region. It is one of the strongest bonds overlaying racial and geographical divergencies, and gives some substance to that elusive region, the Middle East.

The "days of ignorance," of course, were really the days of some of the Middle East's greatest glories. By the time of Muhammad the ancient civilizations had run their course through four thousand years of history and had evolved their own massive cultures.

While these finally disappeared under the onslaught of Islam, they left innumerable, if hidden, marks on the life of the modern Middle East. This is one reason why Islam, for all its core of universal teaching and practice, is not quite the same in every Muslim country. There are certain "cultural chromosomes," to use a biologic analogy, that seem to reappear generation after generation. Shiah Islam, for instance, is partly influenced by the ancient Persian devotion to inherited kingship. The ruler of Iran is still known as "Shah-in-Shah," a name claiming kinship with the ancient Persian title "King-of-Kings" that Darius proudly carved on the rocks of Behistun. Examples of these recurring "cultural chromosomes" are endless. In Cairo, on either side of the Citadel, lie the twin Cities of the Dead. Here Muslims still bury departed family members in the court-yards of tombs built like a house. This is not an Islamic practice but goes back through the centuries to the burial customs of the earliest Egyptians, whose dead slept with the living in one common dwelling. Peasant life in every Muslim country is filled with folklore and folk practices that carry only a thin veneer of Islam. These perpetuate the distant past but are preserved today in ignorance of their origin.

When the Arabs broke out of their desert home in the seventh century to overrun the Middle East, they had little culture of their own beyond immemorial tribal practices. But they did contribute four elements that formed the framework within which Islamic civilization blossomed with such splendor. First was their language, which became a medium of com-munication in all the conquered lands, from Spain in the west to India in the east. Because it was the speech of faith as well as of government it played a part even in regions such as Persia, where Arabic never be-came the tongue of the common people. Scholars, merchants, government officials, and travelers were able to communicate easily with one another, facilitating an intermingling of hitherto diverse cultures.

Then, too, the Arab conquest resulted in a single empire which, although it lasted as a political unity for only a few centuries, brought together the members of many ancient lands. As the Roman Empire formed the political framework in which a Mediterranean culture arose, so the Muslim Empire made it possible for many strands of older Middle Eastern civilizations to be woven together to produce a new Middle East-ern culture.

The third element contributed by the Arabs was a common faith in which men were brothers, despite differences in origin, race, speech, and traditions. During the first few centuries of Islam, the original Arab stock tried to maintain a privileged position. But the dilution of Arab blood, the pressure of the growing number of non-Arab converts, and the equal-itarian concepts of Islam finally produced a society in which the bond of faith overrode the ties of blood.

Finally, the Arab brought a concept of religion as a society, a total way of life. Muhammad not only called men to worship one God and accept his final judgment; he also formed and led a new community. Questions of the conduct of warfare, criminal punishment, commercial practice, inheritance, marriage, and divorce were all governed by religious precept sanctified through divine revelation. "Islam," writes one scholar, "is not a state religion or a religion of the state—it is a religion which is a state." Of course this state (and the society in which it was embedded) was only in embryo when the Arab conquest started. With the impetus to embody Islamic precepts into the total human experience, early Muslims eagerly adopted and absorbed the systems of conquered peoples, finding in them the materials to build their new Muslim world. Diversified cultural influences did not remain merely accidental intrusions into the faith, but were absorbed into its bloodstream to produce a social organism that has ever since been peculiar to Islamic countries.

Within this framework of language, empire, faith, and society, a new and splendid culture emerged. Intellectually, it drew on Greek and Hellenic thought to provide both the theology and philosophy of Muslim scholasticism. In law, it combined the religious teachings of the Koran (Qur'an) and Traditions (Hadith) with legal practices of the conquered countries. This combination is known as the *Sharia,* or Muslim religious law. In architecture it brought together elements from Persian, Byzantine, Armenian, Coptic, Mesopotamian, and Syrian practices to evolve its own distinctive type of building, differing from country to country, yet all governed by a common feeling. In literature, the native song and poetry of the desert tribes was refined and sophisticated to produce a body of lyric verse that was unequaled during the Middle Ages. In science, Greek and Hellenic classics became the basis for original investigation that made the Muslim world the leader in physics, optics, chemistry, mathematics, and geography. Arabic texts were translated into Latin and used in Europe until the dawn of the Renaissance.

This rich culture was not the exclusive product of Muslims. Especially during the earlier period, Christian scholars contributed some of the first translations, and Christian physicians, welcomed by the tolerant caliphs of Baghdad, laid a foundation for Muslim medicine. Jewish scholars also played a significant, if minor role. In contrast to the harsh practices of Christian Europe, Muslims extended to the Jewish minority a tolerance rare in the medieval world. Moses Maimonides, the "second" Moses of Judaism, produced theological and philosophical speculations that permanently affected Christian and Muslim thought.

How far advanced medieval Muslim civilization was in comparison to Europe can be seen by reading accounts of the period. One writer, who fought against the Crusaders, tells of his visits to the Frankish camp and his wonder at the barbaric scenes that met his eyes. At a time when the Muslim world was deciding questions of guilt by recourse to the law courts, the Crusaders used trial by combat—much to the amazement of this cultivated Arab writer, who could not see how brawn in battle determined justice between contestants. He also notes that where Arab physicians treated the sick and wounded with herbs and soothing poultices, European doctors were using a combination of religious charms and brutal surgery that disgusted him.

"But all this is in the past," the modern traveler will object. "I see the Middle East as a backward, underdeveloped area. In what sense can Muslim culture be said to form a living bond in the Middle East today? We, too, once had our closely knit medieval world with its universal tongue and its community of culture. It has vanished. Hasn't Muslim culture likewise gone for good?"

Yes, in many ways it has. The era of Islam's creativity seems to have passed. Since approximately the fourteenth century, it has lived on the traditions of its greatness without producing any outstanding original thinkers, or substantially altering the pattern of its life. Today it is once again in intellectual ferment, but its problem now is not so much to revive and continue its past as to come to terms with the flood of new ideas and practices that are pouring in from the Western world.

There are many reasons why Muslim civilization stagnated. Dynastic rivalries weakened the Islamic world, as did factors of decay inherent in an over-extended empire. The devastating Mongol invasions of the twelfth and thirteenth centuries were an important factor, also. These brutal conquerors destroyed the great centers of Islamic learning in the East—Bokhara, Samarkand, Rai, Baghdad—and put their artisans, craftsmen, and savants to the sword. An Arab historian who describes the sack of Baghdad by the grandson of Ghengis Khan states that most of the inhabitants in the city were slaughtered and that the killing ceased only when the Mongols' stomachs began to turn at the stench of the unburied corpses! From this tidal wave of savagery, the Muslim world never fully recovered. Its universities were torn down, its religious and intellectual leaders slain, its irrigation systems destroyed, and its people left to wander in discouraged impoverishment.

Perhaps it was the shock of invasion that seemed to punish Islam for some mortal sin—Ghengis cleverly played on this theme, representing himself as the "Scourge of God"—that helped the forces of traditionalism to win their final victory. After the fourteenth century the philosophic speculations and scientific inquiries, which had produced such progress in earlier centuries, became heresy, and every attempt to enrich Islamic thought and culture was suspect. Overrun by the Mongols in the East, losing Spain to the Christian world in the West, beset by dynastic rivalries at the heart of its empire, Islam turned in upon itself and lived in strict adherence to the patterns of the past.

A further cause for the decline of medieval greatness was the shifting of world trade routes. So long as the stream of commerce between Europe and the East ran through the Mediterranean, the Middle East was inescapably in the center of the international cultural current. It both received and contributed ideas, but could not, even if it would, insulate itself from what went on beyond its borders. With the rise of the Turks in the fifteenth century and the discoveries of new routes to the Orient around Africa and South America by Europeans who feared Turkish power and resented its high transit duties, this centrality in the cultural currents of the world was lost. What for many centuries had been a great ocean of trade and ideas became a backwater bay into which the life of the world seldom flowed. The Middle East was cut off from the West precisely at the time when the West was entering the period of its own cultural flowering. If the influence of the Renaissance and the beginnings of modern science could have played upon the Middle East, they might have revived its cultural creativity after the shock of the Mongol invasions.

Not until the Suez Canal was opened in 1869 did the trade routes once more pass through the heart of the Muslim world, bringing with them the impact of a new society and the inrush of new ideas. Again Muslim lands were open to the currents of the world—but how different the world from which these currents came! When the Middle East went into eclipse in the fifteenth century, its civilization was of a piece with that of Europe; both were medieval, religious, and scholastic. In their contacts, the Middle East was accepted as at least equal, frequently as superior. But the life of the 1870's that poured through the new Suez trade route was radically changed. Europe itself was losing its religiously oriented culture. Its life was governed by new and complex political ideas, its intellectual world was being formed by experimental science, and its society was undergoing a technological evolution. The once proud traditions of medieval Muslim culture, now ingrown and shorn of their pristine vigor, were no longer accepted by the West. Peoples who had been recognized in twelfth century Europe as intellectual equals were written off in the nineteenth century as merely primitive, backward, and oriental.

The inrush of our times is severely straining the bonds of culture and faith that for so many centuries made the people of the Middle East feel members of a related society. The traditional framework of medieval Islamic life is having to accommodate itself to a new world of ideas, social practices, and political power that repudiates its own basic assumptions. The religious concepts of a medieval society are challenged by the secular outlook of much of the rest of the world. The intellectual content of Muslim scholasticism argues in vain with modern science and pragmatic philosophy. The pattern of Islamic social life is invaded by the radically different practices of the non-Muslim world. Just as the primitive Muslim in the first days of Islam was faced with the problem of adapting and digesting the Hellenistic culture of Mediterranean lands, so the modern Muslim is challenged to adopt and digest the contemporary world culture that so insistently forces its way into his life.

An example of this problem is found in the impact of the new oil industry on the life of Saudi Arabia. Here a complex technical operation of the twentieth century is set amidst the fifteenth century tribal pattern of the Muslim Arab heartland. A money economy has suddenly emerged where barter formerly obtained. The simplest Arab workman in Dahran earns more in a few years than his grandfather saw in an entire lifetime. Motion pictures, unveiled women with bare arms, radios, weekly international air flights, modern hospitals and schools, the demands of industrial efficiency and technical skill—all these are as far from the understanding of the desert Arab as the twentieth century is from the fifteenth. And while an autocratic ruler may forbid Saudis to attend the cinema, order them to be punctual at mosque prayers, and prohibit the importation of liquor, all the power of the state cannot stave off the disintegration of traditional Arab society.

This cultural invasion has been accelerating rapidly during the past century. Not only the oil companies, but missionaries, tourists, travelers, students studying abroad, Point Four technicians, business men, and foreign air bases contribute to the pace of the cultural change. Some of the invasion is deliberate, planned and sponsored by governments who have committed themselves and their countries to the modern Western world. Much is unconscious, however, absorbed from the surrounding atmosphere of modernity or adopted on the utilitarian ground of necessity. One cannot run a modern lathe or ride a bicycle comfortably in skirts—so the traditional (and cool) Arab *ziboon* is cast off in favor of trousers. Urged by the pride of national feeling, Indian women play tennis in saris, but if they were to enter international competition they would have to adopt the simpler garments this vigorous sport demands.

It is naturally in the upper classes that the deepest impact of cultural change is found. Because they engage in international trade and diplomacy, have the leisure and wealth to travel, and are educated in modern universities, the upper classes are becoming thoroughly at home in Western culture. In the process they are often estranged from the mass of their countrymen who still live in a past century. Yet the common people have not escaped the prevalent change, although their clothing and agricultural methods may mislead the tourist into thinking that they are "just like the pictures in the old tombs." Such simple acts as investing in a postal savings bank when Islam forbids giving or taking of interest; being inoculated against plague, although Allah decides the moment of birth and death; or attending a modern village school where the Koran is only an incidental part of the curriculum unconsciously moves the peasant mind from the attitudes of the past. "Men resemble their days more than they resemble their fathers," says an Eastern proverb, and the Muslim of a century ago would be hard pressed to recognize the world in which his descendants now live.

In what sense, then, does the medieval unity of culture and faith form a significant bond in the modern Middle East? First, the feeling of a common faith is still strong and basic. Western travelers, noting the failure of many Europeanized city Muslims to be faithful in prayer and fasting, are tempted to underrate the depth and reality of the religious bond. Their observation would often be true if that bond lay only in personal adherence to theological formulas and ritual practice. But the sense of belonging to a ubiquitous religious community, the conviction that Islam, even when not fully practiced, represents the final form of religion, still supplies a powerful uniting force. In a recent mosque sermon in Beirut, the preacher told his hearers, "We Lebanese Muslims are closer to our Muslim brothers in North Africa, struggling for freedom against the French, than to our Christian fellow citizens in Lebanon." While some of this may be discounted, it bespeaks a sense of belonging that still powerfully affects the different populations of the Middle East.

This sense is not sufficiently strong, however, to recreate the political unity of the earlier Muslim period. Turkey appealed to Islamic feeling during World War I when she called on the world's Muslim peoples to join her in a jihad (religious war) against the Allied powers. But the appeal failed. As one observer has said, "The balloon of pan-Islamic political feeling was blown up until it burst, then came to earth in nationalistic fragments that never can be patched together again." Turkey's secular statehood after World War I, and its faint shadow in the reform movement in Iran, demonstrated that the modern forces of the Middle East were looking beyond their common Muslim heritage to buttress their future development.

In very recent years there has been a certain revival of Islamic political feeling, especially within the Arab world. Non-Arab Muslim states, under the impetus of nationalism, can appeal to their pre-Islamic past for greatness. But for the Arabs, it was Islam that created them as a political power, and national movements in Arab countries often tend to revive Muslim feeling. This does not express itself in effective united political action, but it does create bonds of sympathy with Pakistan in her struggle against India or with the North Africans in their revolt against the French.

The common man, then, even though he may act politically as an Egyptian, Syrian, or Jordanian, feels that the other Middle Eastern peoples are part of his world because they are Muslim, also. Differences in speech, race, and nationality are of lesser account to him when embodied in a brother of the faith. Too, in the face of some form of Western pressure, he shares a common resentment against the non-Muslim world. This is probably less true in Turkey than elsewhere, yet the relaxation of certain prohibitions on Islamic practices (such as allowing the prayer calls and worship in Arabic) shows a widespread popular feeling that all the modernity of Mustafa Kemal and his followers could not erase.

We see that a common pattern of Islamic social practice does continue. It is most evident in village and rural life, since it is in the city that Europeanization naturally takes place first. The basic attitude toward family life, the regulation of such matters of personal conduct as marriage, divorce, and inheritance, the position of traditional religious leaders, and the observance of religious holidays all follow the same pattern whether in Tunisia, Jordan, or Afghanistan. It is true, of course, that few Muslim countries today are governed on a national level by Islamic religious law. Most of them have adopted some modification of the French law code for their criminal and civil legislation, which ultimately will be reflected in changes on a local level. But there is a certain atmosphere common to society within Middle Eastern countries that even the Western traveler recognizes as he moves from country to country among people who all do things in much the same way.

Another living bond of the past that helps create unity across the differences of the Middle East is the memory of Islamic cultural greatness with its long history of intellectual accomplishments. In the first days of nationalistic revival, the Middle Eastern countries tended to turn their backs on their own cultural past in favor of Western culture. But the second stage has often seen a conscious return to past achievements. Within the last half century, both Arabic and Persian literature, history, and culture have undergone a renaissance. Today doctoral dissertations in Eastern universities are being written on classical Muslim authors that a generation ago would have stirred little interest.

Moreover, rapidly growing popular education is introducing an increasing number of Middle Eastern peoples to their own historical and cultural achievements. One of the first acts of Middle Eastern governments when they obtained control of their educational systems after the withdrawal of foreign "advisers" was to insist that every pupil should receive instruction in his own language and history. Up until a few decades ago, much of the education of the Middle East was in foreign schools —either national or missionary—and these sometimes made little attempt to transmit the local culture. Now every foreign school must teach the local language, and frequently the Islamic religion. This will not revive medieval culture, for the curriculum reflects modern European usage. But it does mean that the newly educated generation has more knowledge about their great past than did many of their fathers.

Finally, there is a real sense in which the memory of past political power helps to unite the people of the Middle East. This is not because they are prepared to fight again for a Turkish or Arab empire. Nationalism has eaten too deeply into the fabric of the past to make that possible. But there is a certain psychological strength in the remembrance that Muslim lands were once an important influence in world affairs before they were written off by the West as colonial areas or spheres of influence. The Arab League is partly a reflection of this pride in the past, and while it was unable to lead the Arab world in a united action on such questions as the Baghdad Pact, it did express a community of feeling that cannot be lightly dismissed.

Whether these unifying forces can be strong enough to halt permanently the atomizing effect of nationalism, no one can say. Christianity adapted itself to a divided European world by giving up a political pretension—the Holy Roman Empire—that had never been truly a part of its original and basic faith. But the vision of a single community set over against the non-Muslim world is basic to Islam. Islam itself may have to change if it is to continue to be a bond between people whose political destinies are patterned by the heightened national consciousness that is common to the modern world. As for the unity of medieval culture, this will certainly give way before the pressure of our modern technological civilization.

But if Islam retains its spiritual vitality it may produce a new synthesis of its own past and the modern world that will be as great in its generation as the medieval synthesis was in the twelfth century. Christian apologists are tempted to be too glib in predicting the disappearance of Islam under the impact of the modern world. Their own Christian faith and culture successfully accommodated themselves to the modern age, and it has yet to be shown that Islam cannot do likewise.

PART TWO

STATE AND SOCIETY

1

The Birth of Nations

THE Arabs have a word for it! They call this modern age that is so irresistibly taking possession of their ancient lands the *nahdha. Nahdha* is what you do in the morning after a long night of sleep—"awake," or "sit up and take notice," as our vigorous American idiom puts it. That is just what is happening today in the Middle East. Although geography, people, culture, and faiths continue to be rooted in the ancient past, decisively influencing the present, still something new has been added to the basic elements of traditional life. The something new makes *nahdha* and its Persian and Turkish equivalents both the symbol and the substance of the modern age in the Middle East.

One of the most obvious signs of this awakening is found in the birth of new nations. Fifty years ago there were no independent states of Iraq, Libya, or Syria—to name at random a few of the political units that make up the Middle East today. The sites of these nations and the peoples who compose them are indeed gray with antiquity, but the nations themselves did not exist as political organizations and centers of conscious national life until recent decades. People were known as Libyans, Iraqis, and Syrians in the past, of course, but these names carried no suggestion of self-conscious citizenship in a sovereign state. They indicated where people lived—not the political units to which they belonged.

The implications of this sovereignty and independence are frequently overlooked by the Western world. Accustomed as we are to a century of special arrangements—spheres of influence, protectorates, reserved interests, and mandates—by which Western powers controlled the old Middle East and safeguarded their own interests, it is sometimes difficult to accept the new status of the Middle Eastern states. Egypt's nationalization of the Suez Canal, for instance, may have been both poor diplomacy and questionable ethics, but it was based upon the rights inherent in a sovereign state. These were the same rights evoked when Britain nationalized her railroads, and France her auto industry.

The Middle East is understandably sensitive on this point. When the United States warned of the dangers of a "power vacuum" as a result of the weakening of British influence, Middle Eastern national leaders strongly protested. "We are here," they said. "Our independent nations, fully sovereign in their own territories, cannot be dismissed merely as 'vacuum.' " While it may be questioned that the nations for which they spoke can discharge the same kind of protective responsibility exercised by imperial powers in the past, it is quite true that *they are there* and their presence must be taken into account.

The detailed story of how the birth of modern nations in the Middle East took place is too complex to be presented here. (Anyone seeking to understand the area should read a good modern history, such as George E. Kirk's *A Short History of the Middle East.*) But even a brief survey must begin with the two empires from whose ashes the modern states of the Middle East arose. These are the medieval empire of Islam (sometimes called the Arab Empire) and the Ottoman (Turkish) Empire that succeeded it.

The long procession of earlier imperial powers—Egyptian, Assyrian, Babylonian, Persian, Greek, Roman—left an impressive record, it is true. However, in the consciousness of much of the Middle East, it is chiefly with the rise of Islam that its history really begins. There are occasional resuscitations of ancient pre-Islam days, as when the heralds of an Egyptian university "Field Day" appear in ancient "Pharaonic" costume. But these are often as lacking in contemporary significance as the "Indians" who welcomed the Mayflower II to Plymouth Rock 337 years after the landing of the Pilgrim fathers! Only in Turkey and Iran has a reborn national consciousness turned to its ancient past with serious interest and purpose.

The empire created by the Arab conquests of the seventh century reached its zenith within a hundred years of Muhammad's death. Under the Umayyad dynasty (661-750), the territory from the Indus River and the Aral Sea on the east to the borders of France on the west was ruled as a single state from the Arab capital city of Damascus. It embraced the Persian Empire of the Sassanians, most of the Byzantine possessions of Asia Minor, and the whole of the North African coast. As we have seen, this conquest resulted in much more than the rise of a new political power. It also spread a faith that became a new way of life, forming a

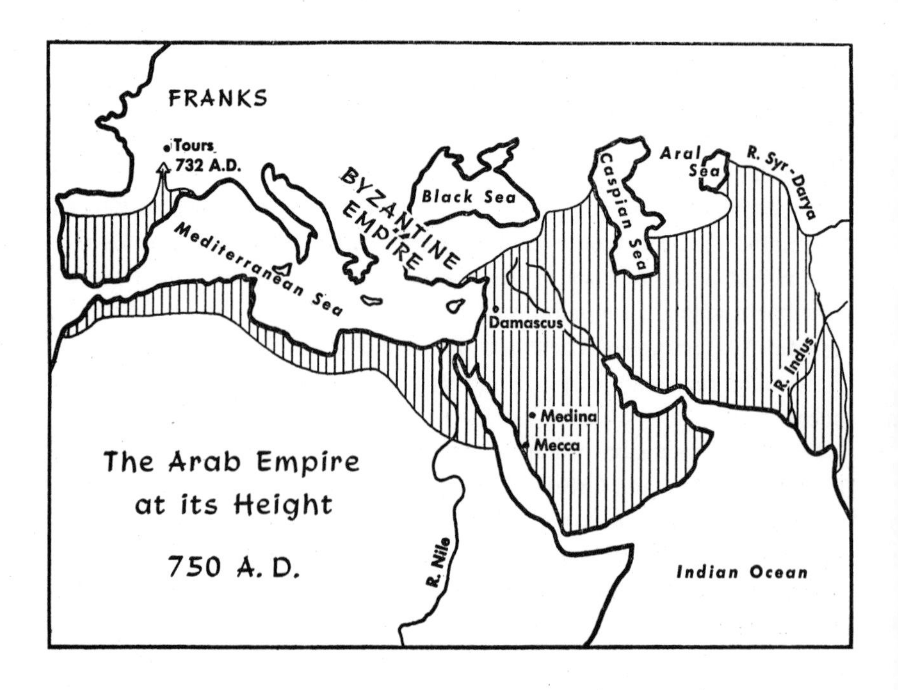

The Arab Empire at its Height 750 A. D.

bond of unity among the many differences of the ancient world; a bond that is still a living fact in the Middle East today. No imperial power before Islam left such a permanent imprint on the life of the people it governed.

The Muslim historian ibn-Khaldun (d. 1406) remarked that empires usually do not last more than three generations. It took a little longer for the Arab Empire to begin its disintegration, although the seeds of destruction were ever present. The old rivalries of pre-Islamic tribal life ultimately reappeared in the ranks of the conquerors; efficient communications were impossible to maintain through a territory nearly five thousand miles in length; and submerged national feeling gradually reacted against the pretensions of Arab rulers. By the beginning of the ninth century the empire was dissolving into a patchwork of local dynasties, each ruling its own territory in real or admitted independence. The caliph in Baghdad formed an ostensible center of loyalty, but he seldom represented effective political control beyond the narrow borders of the Mesopotamian Valley in which the capital city was set.

This fragmentation of political power, for all its interminable and bloody strife, did not destroy the "Muslimness" of the vanishing empire. Spain, North Africa, Egypt, Persia all went their own way. Yet in a sense the Islamic world, like the Holy Roman Empire, lived on in memory and ideal long after its political form had vanished. While no contemporary Middle Eastern leader seriously believes that the restoration of a Muslim empire is feasible, the glory and political importance of that empire forms the soil from which national feeling draws some of its sustenance.

Never again were all the lands encompassed by the Arab Empire restored to a single rule. Spain and the Mediterranean islands were permanently reconquered by Christian Europe. Persia won back its independent existence, and the Moguls absorbed most of India. But in the heart of the Middle East, a new power arose in the fourteenth century that held much of the old Muslim Empire together until our times. Infiltrating the Muslim world as mercenary troops, the central Asian Osmanli Turks (Ottomans) soon established themselves on the southern shores of the

Black Sea. They finally succeeded in doing what the Arab conquerors had never been able to accomplish—overthrowing Constantinople (1453) and bringing Byzantine power to an end. They quickly pushed on south and east to conquer the Fertile Crescent. The Ottomans made themselves masters of North Africa, and drove northward into the Balkans until their advance was halted at the gates of Vienna.

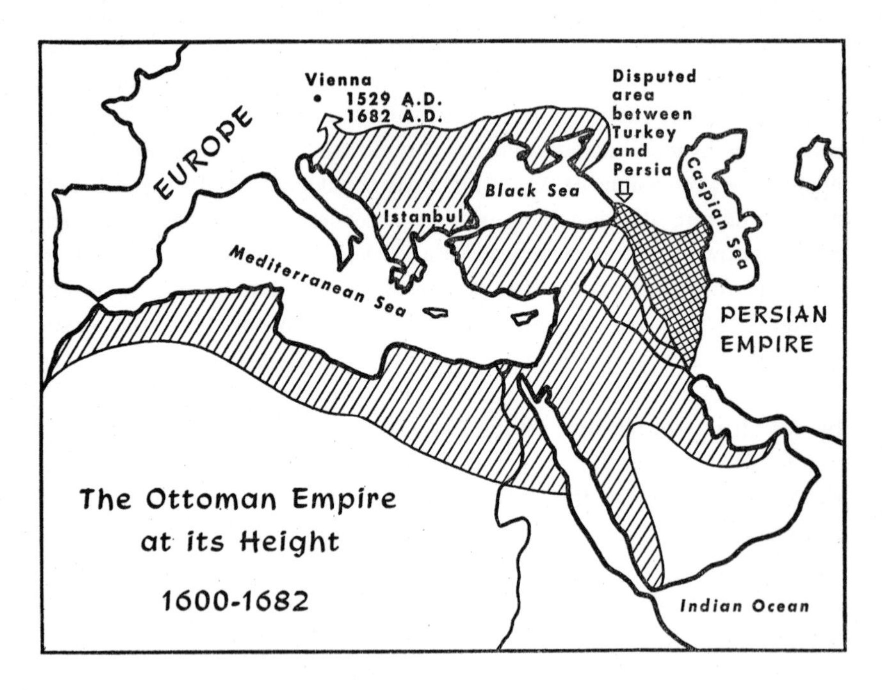

The Ottoman Empire at its Height 1600-1682

At the summit of their power under Suleiman the Magnificent in the sixteenth century, the Turks ruled a vast empire with an estimated forty million inhabitants. Since they adopted Islam as their faith and Islamic civilization as their culture, the Turks appeared to their Muslim subjects to be reviving the vanishing power of Islam itself. By identifying the Turkish sultan with the old office of the caliphate, they were able to evoke religious loyalty and Muslim pride as bonds for their new empire.

It was out of the decay of the Turkish Empire that most of the modern states of the Middle East were born. Revolt and misgovernment from within and the expansive ambitions of European powers from without gradually undermined Turkish rule. Beginning with Greece and Serbia in 1829, the Balkan states gained their independence. At the same time, Turkish power in Africa waned. France seized Algeria in 1830 and Tunisia in 1881, and as a result of the Turco-Italian War of 1911 Italy received most of Libya. Led by the Albanian adventurer, Muhammad Ali, Egypt secured a more or less independent status under Turkish protection in 1841. By the time of World War I, the Turkish Empire was ready to breathe its last—indeed it would have expired decades earlier had not the European powers kept it alive because they could not decide into whose hands the corpse should fall.

The death blow to the Ottoman Empire was administered in the defeat of the Central Powers by the Allies in 1918. In the Treaty of Sevres (1920) Turkey was forced to renounce her sovereignty over the Fertile Crescent and to confirm the previous loss of Egypt and North Africa. For the first time since the seventh century, the control of the Middle East passed into non-Muslim hands.

The Middle Eastern states that came into being as a result of this situation fall into three general categories. There are those that represent revivals of past national entities; those that carved out nationhood chiefly by their own efforts; and those that were created by policies of the West —chiefly under the mandate system.

Turkey and Iran represent revivals of past national entities. By the Treaty of Sevres the Allies intended to divest Turkey of vital independence but keep her as a European-controlled outpost on the Dardanelles, whose strategic importance was being heightened by the ominous rise of Soviet Russia. The national spirit of Turkish patriotism quickly rebelled against this plan. Ignited by a Greek attack on the city of Smyrna, Turkish nationalism took fire under the leadership of an army colonel, Mustafa Kemal, later known as Ataturk.

After defeating the Greeks and forcing a more acceptable peace settlement from the Allies, Turkey turned to her own re-creation. Seldom has a nation so deliberately turned its back on the past and chosen such a radically new pattern for the future. The sultan was deposed and the caliphate abolished. By these acts the nation proclaimed its repudiation both of the Islamic state and the Ottoman imperial history. Turkey became a secular republican state, ruled in theory by a popularly elected national assembly. Despite this democratic framework, Mustafa Kemal was a ruthless dictator, although an able one. After his death the country adopted a two-party system. Under the stress of the postwar years, with their continuous threat from Russia, there has been a tendency to revert to a less democratic government.

Iran has followed a similar path, but with less dramatic results. Through the collapse of Russia during World War I, Britain was left a free hand in Iran, a situation that no self-respecting patriot would be likely to accept for long. As in Turkey (and more recently in Egypt) it was an army officer, Reza Pahlavi, who led the national opposition. Iran already had a constitution and national assembly, and under its young Shah there was at least the outward semblance of a modern constitutional monarchy. Within this framework Reza Pahlavi consolidated his power, finally forcing the national assembly to depose the Shah and elect him as hereditary ruler. He mounted the throne as Reza Shah in 1925, following a path of dictatorship like Mustafa Kemal's.

Under Reza Shah's vigorous and impatient leadership, the country began a rapid program of modernization with a foreign policy aimed principally at decreasing British influence in internal affairs. The national rebirth was interrupted by World War II. Under Allied pressure, Reza Shah abdicated in favor of his son (the present Shah) and a more cooperative and pro-Western government. British and Russian troops occupied the country and Iran became a highly useful transportation route from the head of the Persian Gulf into the back door of Russia. Since the war Iran has resumed her independent life. She made her final gesture of sovereignty by canceling the concessions under which the Anglo-Iranian Oil Company operated and nationalizing petroleum resources and industry. Today she is increasingly allying herself with the West in the struggle against Russia, although she jealously preserves her freedom of action.

Two nations can be said to have achieved national existence largely by their own struggles. These are Egypt and Saudi Arabia. As noted earlier, Egypt forced Turkey to grant her semi-independence during the nineteenth century. This status was practically, though not officially, altered in 1882 when British forces occupied the country as a result of an internal revolutionary movement that threatened both the security of the Suez Canal and the lives of the foreign community. From that date until 1956, the chief target of Egyptian national action has been to force British withdrawal from Egypt and the Sudan.

During World War I, Egypt's tenuous relation to Turkey was ended and the country was proclaimed a British protectorate. With the coming of peace, Egyptian nationalists violently agitated for the end of the occupation, demanding full sovereignty for the country under a constitutional monarchy. Unable to negotiate an acceptable arrangement that would at once protect her interests and meet the demands of the nationalists, Britain unilaterally proclaimed the country an independent kingdom with Sultan Fuad as it first ruler (1922). The independence was not complete, however, for British troops continued to be stationed in the country and certain interests in the Sudan and Canal Zone were "reserved" for future agreement.

In the decades that followed, the extreme nationalists continued to agitate against the British. Usually they were not supported by the throne, which did not favor a strong parliamentary regime in ultranationalist hands. In 1936 a further step toward independence was taken when an Anglo-Egyptian treaty of alliance was signed. This placed the two countries on a more nearly equal basis. Inevitably World War II brought back foreign military occupation and control. Postwar demands for the revision of the 1936 treaty followed, partly on the plea that the United Nations organization superseded all earlier international commitments. Failing in her efforts, Egypt denounced the Anglo-Egyptian treaty and launched a series of guerrilla attacks on the British garrisons in the Canal Zone.

Having aroused the populace, neither Parliament nor the King appeared able to check the popular movement or guide the nation out of the diplomatic impasse it had created for itself. After hectic months when cabinets rose and fell almost by the week, a group of army officers seized power (July, 1952) in a bloodless *coup d'état,* forcing the King to abdicate in favor of his infant son and regency council. A few months later Egypt was proclaimed a republic under the interim rule of a revolutionary council—pending the proclamation of a new constitution. One of the first acts of the new government was to reopen negotiations for British withdrawal from the Canal Zone and a plebiscite to determine the future of the Sudan. With the departure of the last British troops in 1956, Egypt became completely sovereign on her own soil.

In contrast to Egypt, Saudi Arabia was born through an internal struggle rather than in conflict with a Western power. Although it was nominally a part of the old empire, effective Turkish control had been limited to the holy cities of Mecca and Medina and the area surrounding them (known collectively as the Hejaz). During World War I the *Sharif* of Mecca repudiated Turkish rule and threw in his lot with the Allies. Buoyed up by promises of the Western powers, he hoped to create an independent Arab kingdom beyond the confines of the Hejaz. In the peace settlement, however, the *Sharif's* rule was limited to Arabia.

Almost at once a struggle commenced between the ruler of the Hejaz and Abdul Aziz Ibn Saud, a tribal leader heading a movement that had been growing in strength for over a century. Abdul Aziz represented a religious as well as a political rival to the *Sharif.* His followers made up the puritan Muslim movement known as the Wahhabi Brotherhood that was bent on reforming, as well as ruling, Muslim life. After a series of inter-tribal battles, the Wahhabi forces captured the city of Mecca and drove out the *Sharif.* Shortly after, the Kingdom of Saudi Arabia was created, bringing most of the Arabian Peninsula north of Yemen and west of the Persian Gulf sheikhdoms under one rule.

For the first time in centuries the fierce tribal rivalries and interminable raiding of the desert Arabs were brought to a halt by a strong central government. This was largely due to the skill of Abdul Aziz in manipulating tribal support and his wisdom in keeping the Wahhabi Brotherhood as the core of his military and political strength. It was also due to the large oil revenue, which made it possible to support a national police force and communications system. Many feared that Saudi Arabia was only the shadow of a great man that would fade with his death, but the unchallenged succession of the crown prince (the present King Ibn Saud) and the continuance of stable government under his rule seems to attest that a Saudi nation has come into being.

The third group of new Middle Eastern states are those created chiefly by the action of European powers. They include most of North Africa, Pakistan, and the Arab states of the Fertile Crescent. The Fertile Crescent states began as mandates assigned by treaty to France and Great Britain as part of the spoils from the defeat of the Turkish Empire. Iraq and Palestine (which included Transjordan) were placed under British control; Syria and Lebanon under French.

The theory of the mandate was that the mandatory power would be the "big brother" of the new state, assisting it to grow into complete independence under the direction of the League of Nations. Real progress was accomplished under this arrangement. The mandatory powers laid the foundation for civil administration, contributed many physical improvements, and launched such vital public services as education, agriculture, public health, and irrigation. But these actions were naturally closely related to the interests of the mandatory power, and self-government and sovereignty did not develop as rapidly as nationalistic fervor expected. France was particularly loath to let the Levant slip out of her hands, and it took repeated uprisings in Syria and determined pressure by Great Britain and the United States during the closing days of World War II to force the final French withdrawal. Syrian and Lebanese independence did not become a full reality until 1946, when France finally withdrew all her troops.

The British record is somewhat different. Britian terminated the Iraq mandate in 1932, substituting for it a treaty of alliance that bound the two states together. Jordan (which was specifically excluded from Palestine) was gradually developed into a firm Arab ally with generous financial support. After the partition of Palestine, there was a rise in anti-British feeling in Jordan that culminated in the repudiation of a subsidy from Great Britain and the dismissal of the chief British advisers. In the eyes of many Jordanians, their country's independence dates from these acts (1956) rather than from the earlier declaration of statehood made under British auspices.

It is almost impossible to unravel the sad and tangled history of Palestine without being accused of favoritism toward one of the contending parties. Clearly the original mandate involved a hopeless task—that of reconciling the conflicting promises given to Arabs and Zionists during World War I. Each of these groups felt they had sacred rights to the soil of the Holy Land. The Arabs based their claim on nearly thirteen centuries of residence; the Zionists on the ancient links between the country and the Hebrew past. And both pressed their claims on Great Britain, who had promised a home to the Zionists and a state to the Arabs.

Hitler's ghastly persecutions intensified the plight of European Jewry, and immigration into mandated Palestine increased rapidly. This development coincided with the growth of Arab nationalism. Clashes between Jews and Arabs became intense and frequent. At last Great Britain, beset with postwar weakness and wearying of any final acceptable solution, announced its withdrawal from the land. Action by the United Nations followed: Palestine was partitioned between its Arab and Jewish inhabitants with the intent of creating two states, bound in economic union; the city of Jerusalem and its surrounding area were internationalized. From the beginning, the Arabs denied the legal authority or the moral right of the United Nations to dispose of Arab soil, especially without a popular referendum. Therefore they made no effort to set up an Arab state in the part of Palestine assigned to them by the partition action. Instead they appealed to neighboring Arab states for support and as the date for British withdrawal approached, these states began to mass troops on the Palestine border.

Certain Zionist groups also were dissatisfied with the division, which gave them far less than they believed was their due. Terrorist raids and reprisals agitated Palestine as the British prepared for withdrawal and the Zionists prepared for a simultaneous declaration of statehood. Tension culminated in general hostilities with the surrounding Arab countries, who were saved from disaster only by an armistice arranged through the United Nations representative, Dr. Ralph Bunche. Israel emerged from the conflict with nearly 40 per cent more territory than originally had been assigned to her and nearly eight hundred thousand Palestine Arabs were left as refugees in adjacent Arab countries.

The part of Palestine left outside of Israel was quickly absorbed by Jordan with the exception of the Gaza strip, which was occupied by Egypt.

Although beset with unrelenting Arab hostility, Israel has continued her remarkable development and now represents a vigorous national state, well able to defend herself from her neighbors but still financially dependent on gifts and loans from the West. The Arabs refuse to enter into any peace negotiations with Israel until all the United Nations resolutions regarding the original partition and the status of Jerusalem have been implemented. The return of the Arab refugees to their homes and property restitution are other points at issue.

Pakistan is also the creation of a Western power. Originally part of British India, its existence is due to the hostility between the Muslim and Hindu communities that is a heritage from the days of the Moguls. The Congress Party, led by Gandhi, sought a single state in which the various faiths and races of India would cooperate under the common bond of patriotism and national loyalty. Many Muslims feared this would inevitably lead to Hindu dominance and the assignment of a permanent minority status to their community. Their price for agreeing to the end of British rule was the creation of a separate and sovereign Muslim state, centered around the Indus Valley (West Pakistan) but including also a predominantly Muslim area at the head of the Bay of Bengal eleven hundred miles to the east (East Pakistan).

North African states under French influence are still struggling to achieve complete independence. Tunisia and French Morocco have just passed from the status of protectorates, with local rulers under actual French authority, to a form of sovereignty to which France will have a special relation. Algeria, considered as an integral part of France by the mother country, is striving for greater autonomy. The North African situation, particularly in Algeria, has been complicated by the neighboring Arabs who, led by Egypt, support the nationalist movements with arms, propaganda, and political influence.

At stake in the struggle in North Africa are French economic interests and political prestige, as well as the security and status of the French colonists by whose labors these areas have begun Europeanization. Attempts to bring the Algerian situation before the United Nations as a threat to international peace have failed on the French plea that this is an internal concern of France. However, under the pressure of world opinion and the unrelenting agitation and violence of national "liberation movements," the French government is gradually liberalizing its policy. It is probable that Algeria, as well as Tunisia and Morocco, will achieve some form of autonomy within a French sphere of influence.

This record of the birth of nations in the Middle East can be viewed from two sides. One is the pride of the Western world, under whose tutelage most of these new nations were created. There is reason for pride. Probably never before have so many dependent areas emerged into statehood in so short a time through the actions of imperial powers. Admitting all the Western interests that were served through mandates and protectorates, it is still true that most of the states of the Middle East would not exist today in their present form except for France and Great Britain.

But at the same time the West must remember that this pride of achievement is not the last word. For the new nations themselves it is only the first word—the prelude to fufilling the eagerly desired role of sovereign and independent statehood. General Muhammad Naguib of Egypt gave voice to the desire to control their own destinies that is held by every country emerging from the shadow of a Western controlled past. In a speech to his countrymen, he said:

> After having been Iranized, Hellenized, Romanized, and Byzantinized, we were Arabized in the seventh century only to be Ottomanized in the sixteenth. Six centuries later we were Gallicized by Napoleon and Anglicized by a succession of British pro-consuls, including Cromer, Kitchener, and Allenby. Today we are at last in the position to claim the national sovereignty of which we have been so long deprived.

That is *nahdha!*

2

Remaking Society

NAHDHA stands for more than the birth of new nations; it also points to profound changes that are going on within the social structure. Some of these changes are deliberate and planned, such as the pattern of Turkey since World War I, or the constitution proposed for Egypt by the revolutionary council of Gamal Abdel Nasser. Others are the unconscious but inevitable accompaniments of the modern age, with its struggle between the old and the new in ideas, political theories, and technological practices.

The Arabs have a word, too, for the change that awakening brings; they call it a matter of *"nizam."* Some readers may recognize this as the title of a former local Indian ruler, the *Nizam* of Hyderabad. He was called *Nizam* because he ordered his kingdom—for *nizam* means order. There is no exact equivalent in English. *Nizam* embraces also the relations between the different classes of society—all those forces that mold a shapeless mass of humanity together into a single social organism.

It is this question of governmental form and social relationship that lies behind many of the struggles of the Middle East today. The medieval Muslim way of life, with its political presuppositions and social institutions, is gradually giving way to something which, if not better, is at least more modern. The change is certainly incomplete. It takes place at different rates in different countries and affects some levels of society more than others. But in some measure the question of *nizam* is universally present, as any perceptive traveler quickly discovers.

An aspect of *nizam* that has made Western headlines in recent years is the struggle to achieve stability in government. Independence is only the prelude to national life; "what happens next" is the really important thing.

In seeking to understand the reason for the political vigor of the Western world that gained control of their homelands in the nineteenth century, many Europeanized Middle Eastern intellectuals believed that the answer lay in the West's form of government. Constitutionalism under a parliament with cabinet rule not only seemed to promise the East similar success, but offered a way to limit the traditionally autocratic and conservative power of the ruling shahs, sultans, and viceroys. Most Middle Eastern countries consequently established some form of constitutional government when they gained their independence.

The first constitution in the Middle East was established in Iran in 1906. It was accompanied by a national assembly that had the form, if not the political power, of Western parliaments. Strongly opposed by the Shah and some of his supporters, the Iranian constitution was more honored in the breach than in the observance and long represented a goal instead of an achievement. The same was true in Turkey where the "Young Turks" forced from the Sultan a constitution that was likewise ineffective in curtailing his political power. It was clear that these ideas circumscribing the sovereignty of an oriental ruler could not be grafted on to the old form of the oriental state. Something like a national revolution would be necessary before a real change could be made.

That national revolution was made possible in several countries by the disintegration of the Ottoman Empire after World War I. In Turkey and

Iran military movements came to power that overthrew the ruling house and adopted European ideas. In the rest of the Middle East the mandate system gave France and Great Britain control of states just in the making. Part of the plan of the mandatory powers was to introduce and foster forms of constitutional monarchy—as seen in their efforts in Iraq, Jordan, and Egypt. These, it was hoped, would combine some experience of democracy with the stabilizing influence of the "Throne" among a people who needed visible signs of power. Such a plan also offered to the mandatory powers a method of influence and control, since most of the rulers owed their position to the mandate system.

But the record of these parliamentary regimes has not been heartening. Especially since the last war there has been both open and covert revolt against most of the constitutional monarchies. Syria had a string of military *coup d'états,* ending in a restored parliamentary government whose first cabinet lasted a bare six months. In recent months a new military clique has been rising to power and it remains to be seen whether Syria can escape a return to army rule. Iran saw the rise and fall of Mossadegh, in the course of which the throne was nearly overturned. The Egyptian revolution swept aside a century old ruling house to place a military junta at the head of the new republic. Jordan has recently undergone a sharp struggle between radical leadership and the King that fell just short of following the Egyptian revolutionary pattern. Even Iraq, which has had fairly orderly government, has achieved it only through strictly controlled elections guided by the pro-Western Nuri al-Said, often called the "king maker" of the country.

Many Western observers attribute the instability of democratic government to the feudal character of Middle Eastern political leadership. They believe that it is the unwillingness of the hereditary landlord class—and the politicians who represent them—to accept parliamentary rule that prevents constitutionalism from working effectively.

Of course there is some truth in this view. Middle Eastern politicians are blood brothers of politicians everywhere—they identify their personal careers with the interest of the state. The landlord class in the

Middle East is as anxious to survive as the industrial titans of the Western world; of neither can it be expected that they will support a kind of government involving their economic suicide. But to ascribe the struggles and failure of constitutional democracy solely to these causes is a dangerous misreading of reality. What is wrong is not only leaders, but the situation in which they must operate their governments.

The fact is that in most Middle Eastern countries the pre-conditions of democracy in the Western pattern only partially exist. These are at least three: the common man should participate freely in the affairs of his community as a preparation for participation in the affairs of his nation (the New England town meeting); there should be sufficient public information on national issues to allow common people to cast their votes wisely (newspapers, books, radio, television); each citizen should have enough economic freedom to vote without imperiling his livelihood.

These conditions for democratic development are not generally found among the masses of the Middle East. The highly centralized autocratic governments of the past did not foster the growth of local authority nor did the universally low educational level create a demand for it. (Illiteracy is still as high as 85 per cent in some countries.) Moreover the agricultural population, an important segment of the Middle East, is usually composed of small landowners or tenant farmers who are so dependent upon landlord groups that they are disenfranchised to a degree. Nor does the Middle East have the time to develop democratic experience. It is faced with growing pressure to re-make its society *now,* when the twentieth century has already burst upon it. It is clear that the Western democratic prescription cannot be taken without unexpected results. One Middle Eastern historian points out that during the past century the West thought that a "little dose of constitutionalism" would cure most of the ills of colonial people. But that "little dose" has often been the cause of these ills since it has frequently placed governments at the mercy of illiterate mobs whose support was necessary in order to remain in power.

This is well illustrated in Egypt in the rise and fall of the Wafd party. Since World War I, the platform of the Wafd was always "Run out the

British." This was not only the conviction of its leaders, but the slogan also provided an appealing policy that always aroused popular support. However, in implementing this policy in 1950 after the repudiation of the 1936 treaty, the Wafd fell prey to the very mobs its platform had created. Wafd leaders were finally driven from power by General Naguib in the turmoil that brought Gamal Nasser into prominence.

This is the dilemma that political leaders in the Middle East face as they try to meet the desire of their countrymen for more adequate participation in national affairs. Political consciousness has been rapidly spreading from the governing classes of yesterday to the newly conscious middle classes of today. In many countries, also, national systems of education have been introducing the modern world to segments of village life, and the spread of literacy and mass communication has carried Western ideas deeper into the popular mind. Gradually an ever increasing part of each country is identifying itself with the nation and expecting its interests to be represented and served by the national government.

Yet this demand has not been accompanied by the development of an equal competence in individual voters nor of a party system that adequately and honestly organizes their lives. The result is that a popular parliamentary party must, in theory, depend upon a peasant vote. This easily leads to mob appeals for the sake of internal political power, a process that frequently forces the government into ill timed and reckless action. A government in the hands of an inexperienced and unbridled electorate cannot be truly democratic, and may become irresponsible. It is impatience with the confusion engendered in this situation that has led so many of the younger leaders of the Middle East to substitute some form of dictatorial or strong man rule for the constitutional monarchy so recently established.

Here is where the Middle East is seeking a new *nizam*, a new political form. There are those who support a return to the pattern of the medieval Muslim state. Best known of these groups is the once powerful Muslim Brotherhood, which was at the height of its power during and after the Arab-Israeli war. The Brotherhood's appeal was strengthened by the creation of Israel. Its leaders argued, "If the Western world thinks it proper to have a Jewish state in the Middle East, based on a community of religious heritage, why should not we have a Muslim state?"

This view has sometimes enjoyed large popular support and is still the basis of government in Saudi Arabia and Yemen. But few political leaders in Middle Eastern countries accept this position. Nationalism itself is a non-Islamic concept and, when taken to its final conclusion as in Turkey, usually results in a secular government. Moreover, a return to the religious state would bring to the fore the socially and politically conservative forces against which the national leaders of the past decade have been struggling. The latter do not intend to give up either personal power or the hope of the future for the sake of religious loyalty.

Another group looks toward what may be called the "social state," which advocates a mixture of doctrinaire methods as a practical way to control certain aspects of social change. In both Turkey and Iran, the early years of their national revolution were shaped by this dictatorship pattern. Today the revolutionary government in Egypt is following a similar idea. Its new constitution provides a single party government and state control of many aspects of economic life. It is the social state operations of communism, rather than its theoretical roots that appeal to some (especially younger) Middle Eastern intellectuals. The need for a drastic overhaul of society and rapid social change can only be met, they believe, if a strong government takes control of the situation.

Yet the cause of democracy is far from being defeated. In many personal conversations, Middle Eastern political leaders have expressed desires for more democratic procedures. Eventually perhaps governments something like that in the United States will appear. The problem is how to find a political form that will ensure progress and stability yet allow for democratic action. Simply to turn the country over to the mercies of a popular vote by illiterate people is scarcely a feasible answer. Popular education, political experience in running community affairs, and a better economy are all the preludes of a fuller institution of democratic life.

Because of these various factors it is probable that a period of "strong man" rule in the Middle East is inevitable. When talking about dictatorship, it is well to remember that the only dictatorship in modern times that has consciously led on to a functioning democracy is in the Middle East—Turkey. Of course, it took a Mustafa Kemal to do this, backed by national will. As yet there has been no Mustafa Kemal in the Arab world. This is the danger. It is leadership that the Middle East needs above all else. Upon the kind of leadership will depend the gradual recession of the present military tendencies in favor of a more democratic and constitutional life.

Accompanying and related to this struggle for a new pattern of government is a basic change in the composition of the body politic. Through the long ages of the past, Middle Eastern (like Asian) society has been chiefly composed of two parallel yet separated classes. On the bottom stood the common people—farmers, villagers, craftsmen, city merchants. These represented some 70 or 80 per cent of the population and were its most indigenous group, with racial roots running back through centuries of foreign conquest. This class lived a life of its own. Close to the soil, held together by the bonds of custom and religious piety, their lives were governed not so much by politics and conquest as by seed time and harvest.

Over this lower class were the people who belonged to the governing and landowning class. Frequently of foreign blood and culture, they represented the power that controlled the destinies of the state. Their influence was chiefly exercised through their authority to levy taxes and to enroll peasants in military service. But the cohesiveness of the common people was usually too great to allow the governing class to make radical departures from accepted custom. The peasants' attitude was, "You run the government; let us alone to run the land."

But this *nizam* of a dual society is dissolving. Nationalism, probably the most potent idea in Eastern life today, has brought with it the concept that all the people must be included in the national struggle. And national leaders, often against their inclination, are recognizing that if the nations they lead are to be strong and respected in the modern world, the lot of the common people must be better. As a prominent Egyptian leader has remarked, "We cannot expect to be strong and proud and free when half of our people are ignorant, diseased, and poverty-stricken."

To put it differently, the old *excluded* class is now being *included* in the new consciousness of nationhood. In many countries, popular education is being recognized as a responsibility of the state for the first time. In Turkey, Iraq, Egypt, and Iran there has been a remarkable growth in public school systems in the past two decades. Even such a medieval country as Arabia is attempting to launch a national school system. In 1955 the Saudi government employed nearly seven hundred Egyptian teachers to staff its new institutions. When there is added the effective new means of communication—radio, cinema, and newspapers—that reach beyond the schools to the village coffee houses, it is plain why the common people are pressing forward into national consciousness.

There are two important, indeed dramatic, results of this "inclusion of the excluded." One is that the governing class at the top no longer has the complete freedom of action it enjoyed in the past. Then it was possible to have instability at the top without creating serious instability at the bottom; the common people simply went their own way. Affairs of the government were not their business and as long as taxation was not too oppressive nor their traditional way of life seriously threatened, they gave little thought to their governors. But today this is far less true. Constant appeals by various groups for support from the masses, the opening of education to village folk, and the pervading atmosphere of nationalism make it difficult for government leaders to act without taking into serious account the popular attitudes. Today instability in either class produces repercussions on the other. Of course, there are large sections of the population in many areas who are still indifferent to most questions of government policy. But a national crisis of major proportions, such as the Arab-Israeli war or the Anglo-French invasion of Egypt, arouses deep feeling in many parts of the population—a feeling that can make government leaders the captives of mass opinion.

A further result of the gradual amalgamation of the governing and the governed is the demand for social progress. Anyone familiar with the Middle East today knows that beneath the political agitation lies the growing pressure of social discontent. The masses of peasants are gradually awakening to the conviction that their governments both can and should institute needed social reforms.

It is true that the political expression of these social demands does not come spontaneously from the peasants themselves. It is given voice by the politically conscious middle class that has already tasted political power. The middle class is near enough to the peasant group (from which it is being created) to understand and sympathize with it. Peasant discontent is also a potential political weapon that, skilfully organized, can be used to bring new political leaders and classes to power—for good or ill.

Concern for the peasants' condition is reflected in the programs of many of the newer Middle Eastern governments of recent years. One of the first acts of the revolutionary council in Egypt was to limit land ownership sharply and institute a program of land redistribution. Syria attacked the problem of national education; in Iran, Mossadegh tried to force through radical social legislation while distracting the landlords' attention by keeping the British crisis burning at white heat.

The fact is that no Middle Eastern country today, with the exception of some of the states of the Arabian Peninsula, dares overlook the strident popular demand for immediate social improvement. In addition to examples already cited, a considerable amount of social legislation and services has been instituted in various countries. Schools, village social centers, public health clinics, labor laws, land development and distribution plans, cooperative systems are all evidence that the modern Middle East is in some measure responding to its need for social development. Many of these plans may be badly designed or indifferently administered; legislation and talk are often the substitute for accomplishment, but the fact that governments even talk this way—and really do a great deal about it—indicates that a new *nizam* is indeed coming to birth.

That social change is slow in accomplishment is not due simply to insincerity in leadership or lack of will. The basic poverty of Middle Eastern economy imposes a serious and permanent problem. There is a difficulty in financing rapid and large scale improvements that strike at the root of social ills. Above all, there is a lack of trained administrative and technical leadership to implement the complicated process of social regeneration in practical ways. Despite all these difficulties, a new day is dawning in Eastern lands and for the first time in the long centuries of history the welfare of the people is becoming a concern of society.

3

Learning to Live Together

¶ IF THE Middle East were situated in the mountain fastness of central Asia or amid the jungles of South America, it would still have its problems of *nahdha* and *nizam*. For questions posed by changing social patterns and new forms of government accompany national awakening whenever it occurs. But because the Middle East is located where it is—astride three continents where the world's communication routes run through it, it faces a third problem that is peculiar to its situation.

The Arabs have a name for this problem, too. They call it *taqarrib*—drawing near to one another. Some years ago a doughty old Berber warrior, Abd el Krim el Riffi, was asked to lecture in Cairo on North African conditions. Many people expected him to select some such topic as "My Fight Against the French in Morocco," which would reflect his experiences as a rebel leader. Instead he chose the word *taqarrib* as a starting point and discussed "How the People of the World Draw Near to One Another."

"That is the problem that confronts us," said the Arab national leader, "whether it is the French in North Africa, the British in Egypt, or our patriotic struggle against them, the basic question is how we can draw near to one another as neighbors."

Why the Middle East cannot escape this problem is clear. The accident of its geographical location and the character of international life inevitably entangle the area in the affairs of the outside world. Although the lands of the Middle East have long been subject to Western influence, interests, and domination, it has not been simply because the European nations were thirsty for power and national aggrandizement. Imperialism is chiefly a reflection of a nation's struggle for survival. France and Great Britain controlled part of the Middle East because they found their economic and political well-being involved in these distant lands. Today the United States unwillingly assumes responsibilities in this same area because there are international interests at stake that cannot be neglected. This is not to deny that national pride and the prerogatives of leadership have often kept great powers in colonial areas long after their interests have weakened or vanished—as witness the position of Portugal in Goa. But basically imperialism is a response to a need. As long as such need exists there will be a problem of relationship between "dominating" and "dominated" countries.

This is a difficult lesson for Middle Eastern nationalists to learn. Middle Easterners would like to believe that they can maintain the same detachment as people living in countries located in less strategic areas. The fact is that the international character of the Middle East cannot be legislated out of existence by a Middle Eastern parliament nor waived by denouncing a treaty. Its special significance arises from the hard and inescapable facts of location, communications, trade, and politics, and as such it must be realistically faced both by the Middle East and the outside world.

What are these hard facts that have pushed the Middle East into the center of world affairs, creating for it the problem of *taqarrib?* Originally it was Europe's need to maintain communications with its growing overseas colonies and markets. Britain, with interests in Australia, India, and the Far East, made sure that the routes to these areas would be open for her use and secure against the challenge of rival nations. The construction of the Suez Canal brought Britain into the heart of the Middle East and involved her in the occupation of Egypt, through whose territory the canal ran. British control or influence in Cyprus, Palestine, Jordan, Iraq, and the Arabian Peninsula buttressed her position on the Mediterranean-Suez Canal-Red Sea route to the East.

With the weakening of the British imperial system (especially the changed status of India), Middle East communications entered a new role. They were no longer so much a British responsibility in relation to empire, as a vital concern of a number of Western powers. Two world wars emphasized the strategic importance of the Middle East, where victory or defeat could determine the final outcome of a global struggle. Today, when the confusion of the postwar world has settled into a prolonged "cold" conflict, it is equally imperative that the strategic geography of the Middle East be either neutralized or, if possible, bound in alliance to the Western nations and the free world.

To be specific, the threat of Russian world domination has revived and intensified the international importance of Middle Eastern geography. In relation to Russia, the Middle East represents three things. First, it is a target for Russian territorial ambitions. Since the days of Peter the Great, Russia has been steadily moving down on the Middle East and, although the Czar was replaced by the Supreme Soviet, historic Russian interest and policy have not changed. Quite apart from its commitment to communism, Russia is interested in the Middle East for strategic purposes and is actively seeking to win the same kind of influence there that France and Great Britain exercised in the past.

The second Russian interest arises from the Middle East's strategic position for both military and propaganda operations. World War II showed that entrance can be gained to the back door of Russia through the Middle East. Here airfields and missile bases can be pointed toward the Russian heartland without any barrier of satellite states intervening, as in Western Europe. From a propaganda standpoint, these lands situated midway between Africa and Asia form a diffusion center of unusual effectiveness. In Asia, communism is working westward from China. In Africa, it is striving to exploit the discontent in the heart of the continent.

By possessing the Middle East and planting Communist influence there, Russia places herself in a favored position of ideological influence and communication.

Moreover, the Middle East is so vitally connected with Western strategy and political prestige that a Western defeat in the Middle East would have serious repercussions both in Western economy and in the eyes of the uncommitted part of the Eastern world. This in itself is enough to focus Communist interest on the area.

During the early days of World War II, when Germany attempted to insure Russian neutrality, the Russians bargained for a free hand in the Middle East. At the end of the war, when it came time for Russian troops to withdraw from northern Iran, they stubbornly resisted. Their withdrawal was finally brought about by vigorous action of the United Nations. In recent months, Russia has made it abundantly clear that she will move into the Middle East whenever an opportunity opens—as witness her success in Afghanistan, Syria, Egypt, and Yemen.

It is not only Russia's interest in the Middle East that creates and sustains Western concern for the area, however. Equally important is the increasing development of the vast oil resources that are located in Saudi Arabia, Bahrein, Kuwait, Iraq, and Iran. Many people think that Western interest in Middle Eastern oil is inspired only by the selfish and profit-seeking motives of commercial oil companies. The fact is that Middle Eastern petroleum is not primarily important because it produces revenues for share holders. It is important because it is a source of power in a world that is a petroleum-powered world. At the present time, nearly 85 per cent of Western Europe's industry is dependent upon oil for its power and most of this oil comes from the Middle East. It is now estimated that about 66 per cent of the proved petroleum resources of the entire globe are found in and around the head of the Persian Gulf. Obviously, he who controls the oil of the Middle East controls the power supply of much of the free world, especially of Western Europe.

The Suez Canal crisis in 1956 brought home this point. With the temporary dislocation of canal traffic, Europe had either to close its factories or turn to the Western hemisphere for oil imports. While the Americas could supply oil on an emergency basis, to do so permanently would reduce the Western hemisphere's industrial and military potential to a dangerously low level. The fact is that present European economy is based upon the availability of Middle Eastern oil. The loss of access to this source would collapse European economy or subject it to the power that controls Middle Eastern petroleum.

It is clear that the Western world cannot escape the implications of *taqarrib*. The struggle for security and economic well-being inevitably involves the Western world in the life and policy of Middle Eastern lands. But it is often forgotten that the Middle East is likewise inescapably entangled in the affairs of the West. It can no more repudiate a Western connection than the West can repudiate its Middle East connection. The first reason for this is economic. Most of the countries of the Middle East have closer economic relations with Europe than with their sister Eastern states; it is external not internal trade that supports their economy. Egyptian cotton, Syrian wheat, Iranian oil and Afghan sheepskins are all sold to European consumers and provide the foreign exchange that the area needs for the importation of manufactured articles. If the Middle East tried to live in complete economic separation from the outside world, it would quickly feel the pinch of national poverty.

It is from Europe, too, that Middle Eastern countries obtain much of the technical and cultural assistance that they need in their struggle to modernize their lands. Not only is Europe still the training ground for scholars, engineers, and doctors, but Eastern educational systems are largely patterned on European models. The deliberately planned "Europeanization" of cultural life—even of the styles of clothing—demonstrates how consciously the Middle Eastern renaissance has turned toward the European pattern. This is most noticeable in the upper classes, where European culture and languages have taken firm root, becoming almost as indigenous as the classical Turkish, Persian, or Arab cultures of the past.

In addition to economics and culture, the modern Middle East has been partly dependent upon Europe for the development of its political life. It was under the auspices of European states that Iraq, Syria, Lebanon, and Jordan were formed and took their first steps toward independent nationhood. European diplomacy was responsible for the crises that brought rebirth to Turkey, Iran, and Egypt. Whether as a partner or a problem, the states of the Middle East find their political destinies interwoven with those of Europe.

Thus the Middle East and the Western world are bound by *taqarrib*—and neither can easily sever the connection. Unfortunately, this relationship has not found a pattern in the postwar world that satisfies both parties. The West's historic expressions of the connection—colonies, mandates, protectorates, spheres of influence—are no longer acceptable. Yet a complete independence, which most of the new Middle Eastern states propose, is equally unacceptable to the West, since it often fails to make provision for the adequate protection of Western interest. The East fears imperialism in any form. The West believes that independence may mean irresponsibility. Here lies the heart of the problem; how can East and West live together so that the interests of each are reasonably protected?

This problem is made the more difficult because the Middle East now has a power of choice that is new in recent history. Up until World War II there was really only one Europe to which the Middle East could relate itself—the Europe of Great Britain and France. Although this Europe often contained within it national rivalries and struggles for power between contending states, it represented a fairly homogeneous economic, ideological, and political system. The Middle East had no choice but to live in relation to this system. Today, however, there are two Europes—Western and Eastern—that stand in sharp opposition to each other. Not only are they divided by their struggle for world influence, but they represent radically opposed concepts of economic, political, and social organization. The Middle East is free now to do what it could never do before—choose the Europe to which it shall be related. And Western Europe, shorn of its monopoly of Middle Eastern influence, is no longer in a position to force its interests on the area. An Egyptian recently expressed the situation thus: "In the old days, Europe could always back us into a corner since there was no choice between isolation and accepting its dominance. Today, we are no longer in a corner but in a corridor; if the West presses us too far we can always travel down that corridor toward Eastern Europe."

How have the nations of the West and the Middle East attempted to solve this problem of their mutual *taqarrib* in the postwar world? One attempt has been through a system of alliances that would tie Middle Eastern governments militarily and economically to the Western world. Many of these alliances were an outgrowth of the mandatory system. As mandated areas passed into independent nationhood, one of the conditions of their freedom was that they would enter into special treaty relations with the European state formerly responsible for them. Thus Iraq was tied to Great Britain by a treaty of alliance and France moved toward a similar relationship in Syria and Lebanon. Although Egypt was not a mandated territory, the British occupation of the country gave Great Britain the power to insist that she have a privileged relation to the emerging Egyptian state.

After World War II it was difficult to maintain this alliance system. With the growing strength of Eastern nationalism, treaties of special position and privilege were resented by Eastern states and, in some cases, openly repudiated. To substitute for them and safeguard Western interests, there has been an attempt to set up some form of joint defense arrangement or a military partnership between the Western powers and the Middle East.

The first plan was to create MEDO—the Middle East Defense Organization. This embraced the principal Arab states, and France, Great Britain, and Turkey. MEDO was planned with almost no consultation with the Middle Eastern states involved and when it was presented, it was rejected. One of the Arab governments commented, "If this is a partnership of defense, then why were we not involved in the original planning?" Moreover, France, Great Britain, and Turkey were old imperial powers against whom many of the Arab states had struggled to obtain their freedom. Their re-emergence at the head of a military alliance seemed to the Arab world to be merely a new device to cover up an already repudiated arrangement.

A more recent attempt to bring about some form of defense alliance is the Baghdad Pact. Originally this sought to bind together those parts of the Middle East that are adjacent to the Russian border—the northern tier states. Turkey, Iran, and Pakistan readily accepted the arrangement. Although the pact was not widely popular in Iraq, the pro-Western government of that country also accepted the arrangement, thus aligning Iraq with the non-Arab part of the Middle East. It was hoped, indeed freely predicted, that Jordan would also join. It quickly become clear, however, that this hope was based only upon the effectiveness of British pressure. It was in part the attempt to apply this pressure that led to the end of British control in Jordan. While the government of Jordan today is pro-Western, there is little likelihood that it will join the Baghdad Pact.

One reason why Iraq joined the Baghdad Pact was that it had already experienced Communist pressures. During World War II Russian influence backed a separatist movement among the Iraqi Kurds, aimed at setting up an autonomous Kurdish state. Warned of this Russian intention toward Iraq, and bound to the Western world by important oil interests, Iraq braved the resentment of her Arab neighbors to join the pact.

There are those who believe that Saudi Arabia may become a pact member in the near future. Deeply religious in its national life and dependent upon Western oil revenues for its national economy, the Saudi Arabian government has been strong in its opposition to Communist activities in the Arab world. At a conference held at Beirut during the 1956 invasion of Egypt, King Saud of Saudi Arabia sharply reprimanded Nasser for being involved in a situation that might bring Communist "volunteer" fighters into the area.

When King Saud visited this country in 1957, he seemed to have been reassured as to the intention of the United States in the Middle East.

Today Saudi Arabia represents an important pro-Western force in the Arab world. Yet the strength of Pan-Arab feeling in both Iraq and Arabia must not be underestimated. It is significant that both of these countries indicated that they would back Syria against any threatened military action at the time of the Turkish-Syrian crisis—even though Turkey is Iraq's partner in the Baghdad Pact and Saudi Arabia is violently anti-Russian.

Further extension of the alliance concept may be found in the policies known as the Eisenhower Doctrine. They propose a basis on which United States and Middle Eastern powers can unite in opposition to the threat of invasion from Communist-dominated countries. Although no state in the Middle East would willingly acquiesce in its own occupation, the Eisenhower Doctrine found little acceptance. This is partly because some Middle Eastern states do not believe in the threat of overt Communist action. More basically, however, the Arab world resented the implication that its only danger lay in Russia. After the Anglo-French invasion of Egypt, and with the belief that Israel plans to expand her borders in the future, most Arab states feel that the threat of military action rests elsewhere than in Russia. The Eisenhower Doctrine therefore appeared to them to be chiefly designed as a support for the Western position and not a genuine expression of concern for their own territorial integrity.

The Middle East has also tried its own system of alliances. In the past there have been few occasions in which the Arab world and the states north of the mountain barrier have succeeded in organizing themselves for joint action. Since the northern tier states are already tied to the West through the Baghdad Pact, the Arab world has sought its own organization in a regional alliance that would enable it to withstand Western pressure.

The earliest attempt of the Arab states to provide for unified action was through the Arab League. This organization was created during World War II, under the sponsorship of the British. They believed that united political consultation and action might strengthen the cause of the allies, and they therefore encouraged those influences that would draw the Arab world together. Scarcely had the Arab League been launched when it faced a problem that consolidated its position and challenged its utmost capacity. This was the establishment of the state of Israel. Out of the shared resentment against Israel throughout the Arab world, the Arab League was able to evolve common policies and to build up the beginning of a united front toward the Western world.

However, this united front did not prove either solid or enduring. The defeat of the Arab forces by Israel shook confidence in the Arab League as a unifying force and confronted it with political problems that it has thus far been unable to solve. Moreover, it is always difficult to unite states permanently on a negative basis of hatred for a common enemy—as the situation of the Western world in relation to Russia makes clear. The Arab League, too, is beset by the same difficulties that beset the United Nations—differences in national interests and foreign policy that override theoretical loyalty to common action. Many Arabs themselves consider that the Arab League is only a symbol of a deep-seated, but unrealized, Arab unity rather than a political instrument that gives promise of effectively countering Western pressure.

It was partly out of the weakness of the Arab League, and partly from the division of the Arab world by the Baghdad Pact, that Abdel Nasser has attempted to build up what he calls the "third force" or "positive neutralism" in world affairs. When Iraq joined the Baghdad Pact, opposed by her Arab neighbors, Egypt seized the opportunity to use her prestige and influence among neighboring states to gain support for a general policy of neutrality in the East-West struggle. The basis of this was the joint action by Syria, Saudi Arabia, and Egypt, with the hope that Jordan would join. But Egyptian and Syrian involvement in Jordan's internal struggle turned the Jordanian government against the coalition, and growing Communist successes in Egypt and Syria dampened Saudi enthusiasm. Today, Nasser's "positive neutralism" is limited to Egypt and Syria, who have moved toward a federal union.

Yet however unsuccessful the neutrality policies of the Arab League and Egypt have been, there is no doubt that the average Arab, left to his own devices, would seek to escape from taking sides between Russia and the West. After being a battleground in two world wars and seeing how the current East-West struggle seems again to involve the area, it is understandable that the deepest feeling in the Middle East is "a plague on both your houses." One expression of this is the willingness of certain Middle Eastern countries to accept economic assistance from Russia. They argue that such a policy is a necessary counterbalance to Western pressure and only by maintaining a reasonable impartiality about their European connections can they keep clear of being swallowed up by either side.

The matter of *taqarrib* between the West and Middle East cannot be dismissed without reference to the United Nations. When this organization was created, it was hoped by people the world over that it would provide a substitute for older forms of international control. In the Middle East its emergence was hailed with great expectation. At last it seemed that the small, dominated nations could sit down at the council board with their great Western brothers to work out their common problems. But the history of United Nations action in the Middle East has been disappointing. Egypt appealed to the Security Council against the continuance of the 1936 Anglo-Egyptian Treaty, arguing that the United Nations Charter superseded all earlier and "unjust" treaty arrangements. This appeal was not successful; the United Nations refused to take action and directed the contending parties to settle their own difficulties. In this decision, the Middle East learned that when the interests of one of the great powers are at stake, the United Nations is impotent, fearing to anger either the small nation that appealed or the great power that is involved. The failure of the United Nations to take significant action to ease the tension between North African countries and France seems to underscore this point.

But the great blow to United Nations prestige in the eyes of the Middle East was the creation of Israel. It was believed that this creation exceeded the legitimate powers of the world organization and was due to pressure exerted by some of the Western nations. To initial resentment there was added the inability of the United Nations to enforce subsequent resolutions dealing with Arab-Israel disputes. The Arabs include the return of Arab refugees to their homes in Israel, the establishment of the original borders as contained in the partition resolution, and the internationalization of Jerusalem as of first importance. There are also United Nations resolutions arising out of the dispute that the Arab states themselves have not accepted, but these are often overlooked. The history of the United Nations in dealing with the problem that their own action created has greatly weakened any hope in the Arab world that this organization will resolve the conflicting interests and aspirations.

In fairness it must be remembered that the United Nations has also had its successes in the Middle East. It was able to force the Russian withdrawal from Iran and to stop the Israeli invasion of Egypt and the subsequent Anglo-French intervention. Its border commission has dealt patiently, and on the whole successfully, with the innumerable border incidents between Israel and her Arab neighbors. On a number of occasions the Secretary General has used his good offices and official position to lessen tensions between Israel and the Arab states that threatened to erupt in violence. There are still those who believe that the United Nations is the best instrument for reconciling Middle East differences, although they realize that a more effective role probably cannot be played by the organization without the support (or perhaps leadership) of the United States. Whether, in a period of intense cold war, this leadership can safely be exercised is a debatable question, particularly when at the same time Western interests are threatened by Russian policy.

As even this hasty survey of the international situation in the Middle East shows, the problem of *taqarrib* in the Middle East is largely unsolved. In actual political terms there is less security for Western interests than in the period between the world wars. France and Great Britain have lost their dominant positions, yet their withdrawal has not engendered sufficient goodwill for a new relationship to emerge. The United States, which once was regarded as the great hope and ideal of the

Middle East, is now viewed with suspicion, if not with positive hostility. Middle East governments have become effectively sovereign, but they have not developed the strength to assume adequate protection of the major international interests in the area. And on the sidelines there is always Russia—quick and shrewd to profit by Middle Eastern disputes with the West, and relentlessly pursuing her own objective of openly dominating the entire area. If there ever was a time or place where some new approach to the problem of "drawing near to one another as neighbors" was needed, it is in the Middle East—today!

What the approach will be is the task of diplomats and statesmen to determine, but citizens should be informed, too. It is clear that the following factors in the situation must be taken into account:

First is the recognition that military pacts for mutual defense are not sufficient instruments to secure cooperation with the Middle East. That military strength is needed in an area so close to Soviet Russia is undeniable; yet to make such strength the chief tie between East and West has been a failure. MEDO, Baghdad Pact, Eisenhower Doctrine—all have been viewed with deep suspicion. Even those governments that accept them do so with less than complete enthusiasm. To keep the Middle East related to the Western world, the West must do more than provide for the area's defense on Western devised terms.

Second is the fact that the Middle East nations themselves have not solved the problem of their own inter-area *taqarrib*. Not only have the north and south been unable to find a common pattern of action, but within the Arab world there have been misunderstandings, conflicts, and rivalries that have made the Arab world weak in the face of the West and seriously threatened Western interests. While it is inevitable that on many national questions Middle Eastern states will take different views due to their different interests, there are certain major concerns on which united action could benefit them and reassure the West. A more effective area organization in the economic field could utilize oil royalties for regional development and thus strengthen the entire area. The Suez Canal could be approached as an area resource rather than as the national possession of Egypt, and plans could be made for its future development that would involve the oil producing countries dependent upon it. A reasoned and defensible agreement on the general aspects of foreign policy toward the Communist world and the Western world would strengthen the position of the Middle East in international discussions. Until such united measures as these are taken, it is almost inevitable that the West will deal with the Middle East piecemeal to the detriment of both parties.

Third is the recognition by the West that the Middle East is much more concerned about its own internal development than about varied international interests in the area. Here is the root of much misunderstanding. The Western world is deeply conscious that the oil wells, canals, airfields, and strategic geography of the Middle East are essential to its own security and defense. What is forgotten is that the basic interest of the Middle East is not in these physical objects, which form the center of Western concern, but in the task of reshaping its own society. The social awakening and the national development of which they are a part are much more important to many Middle Eastern people than questions of world politics.

To put it differently, we must act not only to protect our stake in the Middle East, but also to give the Middle East a stake in our kind of world. For this it is not enough to offer treaties of defense, Eisenhower doctrines, or guarantees against Communist aggression. What the Middle East needs and wants is assistance in fighting its poverty, developing its economy, and generally in entering the new day of hope and progress that in some form is cherished by all Middle Eastern leaders.

Obviously great difficulties confront the West in meeting these needs. In the end no one can help the Middle Eastern people but the Middle Eastern people themselves. It is not merely a question of contributing money or making generous economic grants. These do not solve the Middle East problem. What the Middle East most needs is a reasonable development of its economic resources, and, particularly, assistance in the training of its people and in the definition of the programs that they will undertake. Unfortunately the West has shown very little of this kind of interest. Even our Point Four program is primarily politically motivated—its chief object being to win friends and influence people in those countries that are threatened by Russia. As an Iranian graduate student said to an American who was discussing technical assistance with him, "Yes, your technical assistance program in Iran is very valuable. The trouble is, we know that you are not here because you are interested in us but because you are afraid of Russia. If the Communist threat were ended tomorrow, you would cease to assist us in building a new society."

Of course the Middle East must be realistic in recognizing the Communist threat and the way in which that threat is activating Western interest in the area. But the West must be equally realistic in recognizing that this threat is not enough to form the basis of *taqarrib*. Only when we are freely able to assist Middle Eastern countries in their internal development, standing with them and for them in their struggle for independence, will the foundation of mutual understanding be laid. Then it will be possible for them and us to live together on some basis of equality and understanding.

PART THREE

MOSQUE AND CHURCH

1

The Call to Prayer

THE Middle East begins its day with a call to prayer. While dawn is still on the horizon, the voice of the muezzin sounds through the stillness, bidding the faithful "come to prayer, come to salvation—for prayer is better than sleep. Rise and pray!" From minaret to minaret the cry passes until the land is ringed with the voice of faith and the reminder that man's waking act should be to bow in reverence before his Maker. No one hearing this call to prayer can fail to be moved by it, for men of every faith recognize and respond to personal piety.

To the Muslim, however, Islam is much more than personal piety. It is the framework of daily life, divinely ordained to mankind as the "straight path, the path of those to whom Thou art gracious, not of those who go astray." (Koran I:5) And that path encompasses more than a personal faith in God surrounded by the ritual of worship. It includes a legal system and a theory of statecraft, and it governs business practices, customs of family life, and international relations. Indeed, the whole round of activities by which man is knit to man in a social organism is inseparable from Islamic beliefs. An individual may neglect ritual worship and repudiate some aspects of theological belief, but he cannot repudiate the matrix of social practice in which Islam has cast his life. Since most of the Middle East is Muslim, the call to prayer and all that it means is one of the most basic and decisive influences shaping the life of the area.

But what does it really mean? To the Christian West, Islam has been both a challenge and an enigma. A challenge, since for centuries it was the faith of political powers in almost continuous conflict with Europe. The original Arab conquests were made at the expense of Christian Byzantium, North Africa, and Spain. In the medieval Crusades there was a protracted and bloody struggle between Christians and Muslims. In the fifteenth and sixteenth centuries, the Ottoman Turks under the banner of the Crescent[1] finally overthrew the Eastern Roman Empire, overran the Balkans, and twice threatened Europe before the gates of Vienna. It is little wonder that the Anglican prayer book once contained a special petition for the conversion of the Turks, or that Luther tried to rally newborn Protestantism against them. Christendom early lost its largest tract of territory—both as a political possession and an area of Christian faith—to the conquering forces of Islam.

Muslims also hardly escape the sense of historic conflict between the Cross and the Crescent. It was the armies of Christian Europe that halted the spread of Islam westward—a catastrophe to the convinced Muslim. Recently the government of Egypt objected to a history text used in a French school in Cairo because it described Charles Martel's victory over the Arabs at the gates of the Pyrenees as having "saved Europe from Islam." "To be historically correct," the Ministry of Education argued, "it should read that this victory deprived Europe of the blessings of Islam." When the spectacular motion picture *The Crusades* was shown in Cairo and Damascus, the Arab press broke out in a flurry of articles caustically recalling the bloody attempts of medieval Europe to invade and conquer the Muslim East in the name of the Cross. Neither Muslim nor Christian can quite forget that for centuries their nations were locked in strife.

[1] The crescent was adopted as an emblem by the Turks after the fall of Constantinople in 1453. Popular usage regards the crescent as a symbol of Islamic political power.

Islam is also an enigma to the Christian West. The only great world religion to postdate Christianity, it has proudly and insistently proclaimed the superiority and finality of its faith. Yet much of that faith is akin to Christian convictions—the uncompromising belief in one God, the revelation of his will through inspired scripture, the personal immortality of the believer, the final day of God's judgment, the mission and message of the Old Testament prophets, the divine calling of Jesus himself. With some notable exceptions, the moral teachings of the Koran breathe the atmosphere of Deuteronomy and sound familiar to Christian ears. From almost every point of view, Islam is closer to Christianity than any other religion except Judaism.

One of the earliest Christian explanations treated Islam as a Christian heresy. This was propounded in the eighth century by an Eastern church father, John of Damascus—known to Western churchgoers for his hymn, "The Day of Resurrection." Toynbee in his *The World and the West* has recently suggested the same view. The argument is that Muhammad adopted and made central to his message certain aspects of Christian belief, notably monotheism, but left out, as is done in all heresies, counterbalancing and vital truths.

Another Christian explanation, simpler and more popular, is that Muhammad was consciously an impostor who drew on prevailing Christian and Jewish religious ideas to build a new religion for the sake of political power. One of the earliest studies of Islam in English, published in London in 1697, called Muhammad "that clever impostor" and represented him as a sly and ambitious Arab leader bent on furthering his own career. Christian tradition in the Middle East, without any historical support, has even named the monk who is said to have given Muhammad the religious instructions on which his ideas were built.

Such explanations say little beyond the fact that there is obviously a community of ideas between the three religions of Semitic origin—Judaism, Christianity, and Islam. Modern studies in the history of ideas reveal the true situation. Pre-Islamic Arabia was penetrated by certain Judeo-Christian influences, some coming from countries beyond its borders, some from scattered Jewish and Christian communities within. Jewish and Christian Scriptures and Apochrypha were known; stories and vocabulary from them were apparently used by others before Muhammad. These formed part of the raw material for the Prophet's religious experience. So while such thought forms were not original with Muhammad himself, he filled them with his own meaning and combined them to produce a new faith, Islam. It is thus no more possible to understand Islam simply as warmed-over religious ideas from the past than it is to understand Christianity in similar terms. And if Muhammad is accused of consciously, perhaps cynically, inventing a new faith, the same allegation has been brought against the Apostle Paul by some people who allege that he transmuted the simple Jewish beliefs of Jesus into a new religion by adding to them the form and content of Eastern mystery cults.

The fact is that no achievement can be entirely explained or evaluated in terms of its historic origin, else the science of medicine would be suspect because it originally grew out of primitive magical practices. If we are to understand Islam, we must lay aside both its conflicts with the Christian West and its relation to our own beliefs and consider it first as a living faith, to which more than 365 million people throughout the world turn for spiritual guidance. "What does Islam mean to the Muslim; to what does he feel the call to prayer calls him?" This is our concern.

To give a complete and detailed description of Islam is a task as vast and intricate as similarly to describe Christianity. Like Christianity, Islam has an extensive theology, supported by a variety of philosophical systems. Like Christianity, it has a multiplicity of sects produced both by doctrinal differences and the accidents of history. And like Christianity, it runs the gamut of religious outlooks, from the crude and superstitious beliefs of simple people to the rational and philosophical convictions of the educated. Moreover Islam, like Christianity, has produced an impressive culture and social system that is both the reflection of its spiritual vision and a force reacting on its own faith. All these factors would have to be understood and appraised to know adequately what Islam means.

Just as Christianity, for all its elaboration, rests upon certain basic and simply stated convictions, so Islam can be reduced to a core of central beliefs and practices that are professed in some form by all who bear the name Muslim.

Foremost of these beliefs and practices is the name given the religion itself. Islam was Muhammad's own term for the faith he brought, and it is the word that sums up for his followers the essential character of their religion. Islam means "submission" or "surrender." It suggests that the religious life is first of all a life based upon the acceptance of and obedience to God's way—in contrast to the way of men.

At its origin, Islam had a specific and contemporary meaning. When Muhammad began his mission, he found his countrymen in Mecca leading careless and dissolute lives, following a religion of crude polytheism and given to primitive idol worship. To them he preached God's judgment on idolatry and immorality and, like many prophets before him, warned men to flee from "the wrath to come" by abandoning their foolish ways and acknowledging Allah, the one true God. As this early and simple message became more elaborate, finally encompassing a complete theology and social practice, the content of Islam became more complex. Ultimately it comprehended a fully ordered personal, social, and political life embodying God's revealed will for mankind—a life doubtless more total and complete in theory than in practice. Whatever disagreement there may be between theory and practice, however, Islam always emphasizes that the heart of religion lies in man's obedience to the way of life God has set before him.

Those who accepted Muhammad's message he called Muslims, meaning "the surrendered ones." Westerners often incorrectly call the followers of Islam "Muhammadans" and their religion "Muhammadism."

Islam means more than simple surrender to what any man conceives to be the will of God; it means surrender to the particular will of God announced by Muhammad. This, of course, means accepting the role of Muhammad as a divinely inspired prophet. However Christian theology or modern psychology may explain it, there can be no doubt that Muhammad considered and represented himself to be the instrument chosen by God to reveal his final will to men. Sometimes he was very simple in his claims; "I only warn you" he cautioned his fellow Arabs. (Koran, XXI:46) Yet at other times he equated his mission with the very core of religion, placing "belief in God" and "belief in His apostle" on an equality.

After Muhammad's flight (*hijrah*) from Mecca, he and his followers founded a rival community in Medina. As the practical administrator of community affairs, he assumed a social role. He also was involved in military leadership, since the Muslims were in almost continuous conflict with their pagan brothers. Moreover, Muhammad's prophetship took on political implications, for to acknowledge his religious mission was to accept his military and social leadership. When at last Muhammad returned in triumph to his native city, he established a rule as well as a faith—or rather a faith that included a rule.

Although Muhammad made no special claims for himself except his role as a religious leader, the pious Muslim generations who followed developed an exalted description of him that almost rivals some aspects of the Christian attitude toward Jesus. In addition to being "the last and the seal of the prophets," Muhammad is said to have been sinless, perfect, the divine revelation of what humanity in its fullness ought to be. In some sects this has been expanded to include a form of pre-existence and an intercessory mission in heaven.

Muhammad's role as a prophet is inseparable from the utterances by which God made known his will through him. These utterances are gathered together in the sacred scripture of Islam, the Koran (more correctly transliterated Qur'an). Koran means "recitations." In Islamic usage it indicates the compilation of Muhammad's words when he believed himself to be under the spell of divine inspiration. These sayings, given in what we would call rhymed prose, were often memorized by their hearers; some of them were even written down during Muhammad's lifetime. Shortly after his death what was remembered and written was collected to form the text of the written Koran.

The Koran is a volume about the size of the New Testament. It is composed of 114 chapters (called suras) of varying length, each being named from some verse or incident in the text. In content they represent sermons preached by the Prophet and legislation enjoined by him when questions of faith and practice arose. For the Muslim, the Koran represents not only the supreme book in the Arabic language, but the most majestic writing of the ages. It is the "sign" and "miracle" to which Muhammad himself pointed when proof of his prophetic mission was demanded. In translation, the Koran seems to be dull and uninspiring, but in its original Arabic it has a sonorous cadence that is very moving—occasionally reminiscent of some of the great passages of the Psalms and Isaiah.

The text of the Koran, represented as divine inspiration, was accepted as such by those who heard and followed Muhammad. As long as the Prophet was alive, he was the living font of guidance. It was only after his death, when the "door of revelation" had been closed, that the written Koran became the foundation of Muslim faith and practice. Gradually a theological view of the Koran was developed that is accepted in some form by the Muslim community today. Islam's theory negates the personal role of Muhammad. The words of the Koran are God's words and Muhammad was only the mouthpiece. The words existed in some form since all eternity (for many Muslims the Koran is uncreated and thus represents an eternal aspect of the Divine). It was "sent down" from Heaven to Muhammad at the appropriate time but contains truth that is timeless because it always existed, either in the mind of God (as some philosophers maintain) or written on a mystically understood "tablet" which is part of the eternal order. The Koran therefore has an absolute authority for the Muslim. Its very words and grammar, as well as its meaning, have a divine origin and when the Muslim hears or reads it he feels that God himself is speaking to him.

From the Koran and its interpretation, the Muslim learns that the center of his faith is an unquestioning and unswerving belief in one—and only one—deity, to whom there is no partner. To this is added, as already noted, acceptance of the prophetic role of Muhammad (and other prophets) and the holy books (supremely the Koran, then earlier scriptures). Other articles of faith include belief in the last judgment, in predestination, and in angelic beings both good and evil.

To the articles of faith are added the five fundamental duties required of every Muslim. These are (1) the repetition of the creed "There is no God but God and Muhammad is the apostle of God," (2) the performance of worship or ritual prayer (five times daily, but not so specified in the Koran), (3) fasting from daybreak to sunset during the month of Ramadan, (4) payment of legal alms for the support of the poor, and (5) making a pilgrimage to Mecca once during a lifetime.

Of course Muslim life does not stop with these duties. The Koran provides many warnings and moral exhortations that the believer should heed and follow in patterning his life. Care of orphans, honesty in business transactions, kindness to brothers in the faith, just treatment of wives and children are all enjoined in the Koran. Muhammad was appealed to by his followers on many questions besides religious beliefs and most of his answers were given as divine revelations.

While the Koran gives guidance in many specifics of conduct, it obviously could not answer all the questions of faith and practice that later generations of Muslims would ask. Therefore it is supplemented by the *hadith,* traditions. Since Muhammad was believed to be divinely inspired, what he did as well as what he said assumed significance, and accounts of his activities were collected to form the traditions.

Working with these two basic sources, the Koran and the *hadith,* Muslim philosophers and jurists of later ages evolved an elaborate system of morals and laws to govern the Muslim community.

As a result of this interpretative and additive process, the original, simple, and limited social message of Muhammad has been expanded to provide the framework for a complex society. Doubtless Muhammad, like many another founder of religion, would stand amazed at what is done in his name. Yet for the medieval and modern Muslim, Islam has provided a practical answer to many of life's most detailed questions. To emphasize again, Islam is a *total* way of life—personal, social, economic, political.

This brief description of what a Muslim believes is important in identifying his faith. It does not explain satisfactorily the reason for the vitality of Islam. For Islam is vital. No faith to which some 365 million people turn for guidance and that has lasted aggressively through thirteen centuries can be written off as insignificant or decadent. In birth and death, in poverty and defeat, men have found and still find strength and stability in this faith. How? What experiences found in his religion give meaning to the Muslim's life?

First is the insistent, inescapable fact of God. In saying "There is no God but God" the Muslim not only denies idolatry and polytheism, but affirms that in the end God is the one agent that undergirds and acts through all creation. It is not uncommon to see the name Allah written on the dashboard of a taxi or over the counter of a bazaar shop—for Allah is the most basic reality of life. Because Islam has no priesthood or mediator, each man feels himself to be in the direct and inescapable presence of God. Although philosophy and theology have elaborated this in complex and intellectual terms, to the average Muslim, God *is*.

The fact that Islam is not complicated by metaphysical subtleties is one reason why it has appealed so widely. Contrary to popular belief, the largest accessions to the Muslim faith were not made by the sword (as Sir Thomas Arnold's *Preaching of Islam* shows) but by the proclamation of its uncomplicated message. "Simply believe in God—ask no questions about him" is not an unfair summary.

A second value that has given vitality to Islam is its practical experience of brotherhood. When Muhammad first announced his message he faced the opposition of the leading tribal families of Meccan society. Consciously, and as a part of the divine revelation, he set himself against the social snobbery of Arab society, substituting the bond of faith for the bond of blood.

The early Arab community did not take kindly to this equalitarianism. After Muhammad's death the old pre-Islamic tribal prides and jealousies reappeared. As Islam moved out across the world, the Arab aristocracy attempted to keep a privileged position. For some two centuries the matter was fought out, until at last Islam was committed to a principle of a brotherhood beyond race, language, or color.

Islam is often criticized because this brotherhood is a "brotherhood of the faith" and not "a brotherhood of all men." The criticism is founded on fact. As the Muslim looks out on the rest of humanity, he feels himself to be in the privileged position of one who has accepted the only true way. Moreover, the sense of world mission in Islam—sometimes identified with military conquest—inhibits the growth of a fraternity beyond the bonds of religion. Yet within Islam the brotherhood is strong and real. The beggar from the streets, the tradesman from the bazaar, and the wealthy merchant from his counting house stand side by side in the mosque and bow in prayer together. The Muslim's sense of kinship also binds him to those far separated in race and culture. This even holds in the realm of color, where the Christian West has often and lamentably failed. Color, as such, is no divider of persons in Muslim society.

The meaning of this brotherhood was especially significant in the Middle East, where Islam was born. The Middle East is inherently a medley of peoples, cultures, races, and faiths that have little in common. Across this divided and suspicious world, Islam swept with a new and generous concept of human relations. Spaniards, Berbers, Egyptians, Turks, Persians, Arabs found a common experience in which they were accepted as members of the body of the faithful and not as warring and hostile societies in historic conflict. One of the enduring symbols of this brotherhood is the yearly pilgrimage to Mecca.

Another appeal of Islam lies in the practicality and directness of its moral system. Few people enjoy working out for themselves an acceptable code of life. They want to be told—and told in reasonable and practicable terms—what it is that "the Lord thy God doth require of thee."[1] Islam supplies very specific answers. The intimate and daily rou-

[1] King James Version.

tine of family life no less than the great observances of religion are precisely prescribed. Human actions are catalogued as "forbidden," "not advisable," "neutral," "recommended," "enjoined." Under these headings most of the individual's moral dilemmas can be answered.

Moreover, the practical precepts of Islam are based upon a shrewd and realistic appraisal of human nature. Muhammad was a politician as well as a prophet, and being a politician he sought practical answers to the problems of his followers. In general, the Koran sees and accepts human nature as it is, then tries to refine that human nature through reasonable improvement. A good example can be found in the way in which Muhammad dealt with the position of women in his day. In pre-Islamic Arabia, polygamy was unlimited. Women had few rights and were often regarded as chattels to be inherited from father to son. Muhammad changed this, but the changes he introduced appeared reasonable and possible of acceptance in his seventh century society. He limited polygamy, but did not wipe it out. He gave women legal and marital rights, but did not place them on a full equality with men. He enjoined affection and justice in treatment of wives without displacing the man as the ruler of the household. When such legislation is measured against the position of women in the twentieth century Western world, it appears to be medieval, despite its advance over seventh century Arabia.

Serious objection can be raised against any system that tries to reduce the good life to a code of specific practices—especially when these are considered to be divinely ordained. Human life does not stand still, and no single mind in any generation has ever been sufficiently far-sighted to legislate for all possible conditions in all possible future ages. Yet undeniably, many people want such legislation and the clear-cut and realistic duties Islam requires of its adherents has given it great strength.

Perhaps these values could be summarized by saying that Islam enshrines one of the permanent religious interpretations of human experience. God is one, God is powerful, God is intelligent, God is the ultimate basis of all being. To this is added the practical view of human nature already described. "God has not commanded what is difficult for you," says the Koran, "but what is easy." Moral duties are based upon life as men now live it, but refined and guided under the direction of wise and realistic moral precepts. "From this point of view," one Christian theologian has said, "many Christians are really Muslims. This is a popular religion in our day!"

Whether this religious system and its values are what the Muslim claims them to be—the final revelation of God's will to men—is quite another question. What we are concerned with here is to understand that Islam makes sense to those who profess it and provides a powerful and practicable basis on which to build their lives and regulate their society.

2

The Stubborn Remnants

¶ THE call to prayer from the mosque is the major influence in the religious life of the Middle East, but there are also significant, if very small, Christian communities scattered through the area—stubborn remnants of the days before Islam. Only in Lebanon do Christians even approximate a majority.

It might be supposed that centuries of minority status within the enveloping Muslim world would have driven these Christian groups closer together and lessened their doctrinal differences, some of which go back to the earliest centuries of the Christian era. But the opposite is too frequently true. Individual communities pursue a separate life and rarely cooperate effectively with other Christian groups, especially those beyond their national borders. Perhaps this is the inevitable result of the long struggle to survive, for survival was accomplished only by passionate loyalty to their Christian past maintained by each separate community engulfed by Islam. To preserve that community intact in its worship, legal position, historic privileges, and social practices has been the principal object of Eastern Christianity through the centuries. Indeed, there was scarcely any other approach possible since the religious minorities did not enjoy all the rights and protections given by the state to the majority. Christian groups consequently often display a narrow and unreasoning loyalty to the past, suspicion of theological and administrative change, and fear of any innovation that might imperil the working arrangements with the Muslim community in which the Christians must dwell.

The indigenous Christian sects of the Middle East are differentiated outwardly by the language of their liturgy and the peculiarities of their theology. All stand within the fold of the Orthodox (Eastern) tradition of Christianity as opposed to the Roman Catholic (Western) tradition. Their administration is under the authority of a patriarch (bishop) who claims apostolic succession. In the eyes of their churches, the patriarchs are the true successors of Peter, and the pope is only a Western interloper without either historic or theological justification. Some years ago, when the Pope invited Eastern churches to return to communion with Rome, the Patriarch of one responded with an invitation to the Pope and his erring followers to return to the See of Antioch—the original and scriptural scene of Peter's first Gentile labors!

The use of differing liturgical languages (Coptic, Syriac, Armenian, Greek, Arabic) and varying doctrinal standards concerning the person of Christ are the official marks of Eastern sectarianism, but the historic reasons for such divisions were frequently national rather than theological. A particular doctrine was often espoused and defended, not because the mass of the clergy were deeply convinced of its truth, but because it represented a symbol of national feeling against the domination of a foreign group. This was true in Egypt, for example, where political resistance to the Greek rule of Byzantium took the form of supporting Egyptian theologians against the Greek theologians. Disputes continued until 451 when a definite schism was created by the Council of Chalcedon. The result was the establishment of the Coptic, which means Egyptian, Church as the national church of ancient Egypt. Technically heretical in character from the standpoint of the mainstream of Christian beliefs (Orthodox, Roman, and Protestant), it is best understood as the protest of the Egyptians against attempts to enforce Greek beliefs.

The Christian communities of the Middle East can be separated into four classifications. First is the Orthodox group. This division represents remnants of the official faith of the Byzantine Empire at the time it was overrun by the Arabs in the seventh century. In Egypt and Turkey, Eastern Orthodoxy is found chiefly among the Greek colonies, many of which have lived there for centuries. In Palestine, Lebanon, and Syria there are Arabic-speaking Orthodox Christians who trace their beginnings back to native, pre-Islamic communities. East of the Mediterranean seacoast countries there are no Orthodox groups except for scattered immigrants, since Byzantine power never controlled this area.

The second group—and the largest—is difficult to name. Strictly speaking they are theological variants of Eastern Orthodoxy, although their origin was often national rather than doctrinal. The immediate cause of their differences was the difficulty of the ancient church in defining the exact nature of Christ so as to explain and include both his human and divine character. At the Council of Nicea in 325, which was the first effort of the ancient church to clarify the nature of Christ, and in Chalcedon in 451, two extreme views were repudiated. However, some "national" Christian leaders continued to cling to their own beliefs. One group, known as Nestorians, so separated the divine and human nature in Christ that there tended to emerge two entities—the human, historical Jesus and the eternal, divine Word (logos). Although the councils declared this view to be heretical, it persisted in groups on the fringe of the Byzantine Empire. Nestorianism was a strongly missionary faith and spread through ancient Persia and even to China and India. Today it is represented by the Assyrian or Church of the East communities in Iraq, Syria, and Iran.

Opposite the Nestorians stand the Monophysites. This name is derived from the Greek word meaning "of one nature" and designates a belief that, although Jesus was both human and divine, the two aspects of his existence were contained in one composite nature. While Nestorianism implied a human Jesus without a truly eternal nature, Monophysitism tended to view Jesus as so divine that he had no real humanity.

The Monophysite group includes the Coptic Church of Egypt, the Church of Ethiopia, the Syrian (Jacobite) Church (principally in Iraq), and the Armenian Church. Although of similar theological persuasion, these churches are not organized into a single group and look with some suspicion upon one another. Each is really the remnant of a national church, as some of their names suggest.

Adherents from both the Orthodox and separatist communities form the third section of Eastern Christianity—the Uniate churches. These are composed of sections of the ancient churches that in time accepted the rule of the papacy, repudiating the heretical portions of their theology. The Roman Church never acquiesced in the existence of Eastern churches outside the authority of the pope. Ever since the schism between Roman and Eastern Christianity in 1054, one of the principal objectives of Roman Catholic activity in the Middle East has been the ingathering of Eastern communions. This has led to Roman Catholic branches of most churches. Today there are Greek Catholic, Coptic Catholic, Armenian Catholic, Chaldean (Nestorian Catholic), and Maronite (Lebanese Catholic) Churches. Together they are called "Uniate" because they "united" with the Roman Church.

Although accepting the papacy these Uniate churches retain their own liturgies, ceremonies, and rites. In many, priests are permitted to marry, this being ancient Eastern custom. Between them and their parent Eastern communities there is often deep and bitter feeling, since in "going over to Rome" they have repudiated both a national and a religious past. So deep is the feeling that many of the Eastern churches refuse to use the Western calendar for the Christian feasts, because this was evolved under the papacy. Consequently, there are two Christmases and two Easters in most Middle Eastern countries.

The fourth group of Eastern Christians comprises the various Protestant denominations, each the result of Western missionary work.

The Reformation did not touch Eastern Christianity. From one point of view, Eastern Christianity had no need of the Reformation, at least in terms of the immediate situation in the sixteenth century. The abuses against which the Reformation first protested—indulgences, papal power, the political ambitions of the papacy, the seclusion of the Bible—did not exist in the East. Moreover, Eastern church groups were naturally not represented at the councils that tried to deal with the Reformation controversy. For these reasons Protestantism has always seemed to Eastern eyes a purely Western phenomenon, aimed at the Roman Catholic Church and *as such* appreciated as a protest against Roman power. But when Protestantism was introduced into the Middle East and took as its foil the Eastern Church, it became a movement to be feared and resisted—as "Western" and heretical as Romanism itself.

To be fair to the early missionaries, their first object was to convert Muslims, not Eastern Christians. But some missionaries felt that it was the *Eastern* Christian who should deal with his own non-Christian neighbor; that his spiritual life should be revived and strengthened to that end. Moreover, work among Muslims was extremely difficult, since they showed great resistance to evangelization. Under these circumstances, missionaries not unnaturally turned to and welcomed the inquiries of local Christians. Rarely did the missionary deliberately campaign to detach the Eastern Christian from his historic church. It was hoped that through better training of priests and a more enlightened use of the Bible, the ancient churches could be leavened from within. Often, however, these churches turned against their Protestant minded members because of their criticisms. The Protestant sympathizers censured the actions and ignorance of the clergy, compared ancient rites with the simplicity of the New Testament, and demanded such innovations as Sunday schools and the use of the vernacular in services. Driven out of their churches by their own leaders, such people turned to the missionaries for guidance and comfort, with the result that Protestant churches were finally formed.

These churches represent a variety of Western cultural backgrounds and denominations (German, English, Scottish, Scandinavian, American). Even when they have become indigenous in organization (as the newly formed Evangelical Church in Egypt) they bear a strong Western stamp. Their form of worship is typically Western Protestant, with chief emphasis on the sermon. Their music is Western, with translations of familiar hymns, set to Western tunes. Their theology is drawn from the doctrinal standards of their Western mother churches. There is almost nothing about them to stamp them as "Eastern" except the background of the worshipers. When the Reformation started in Europe, it made much use of familiar medieval Christian forms, as witness the worship of the Lutheran and Anglican Churches. To many simple people, this doubtless formed a bridge over which they gradually passed into Protestantism without too violent a sense of separation from the heritage of the past. But this process was not repeated in the East. There nineteenth century Protestantism, itself four centuries old in the West, came as a sharp break with the Eastern tradition—a handicap that has never been entirely overcome.

What is the relation of these "stubborn remnants" of a once dominant faith to the engulfing Muslim community? The answer varies with the type of relationship under consideration. Culturally, Eastern Christians have played an honorable part within the great developments of Islamic civilization. In the early centuries Christian scholars were prominent in transmitting classical learning to the rising Muslim community. In recent times, Christian Arab scholars in Lebanon played a leading role in fostering an Arab renaissance, producing some of its first works—as George Antonius has shown in his carefully documented *Arab Awakening.* Although frequently shut out of the highest posts in government, Christians have occupied many secondary posts, being on the whole (until recent times) better educated than the Muslim majority and showing all the financial skill and ambition that sometimes characterizes minority groups. In the various modern nationalistic movements of the Arab world (especially in Palestine and Egypt), Christians have stood with their Muslim brethren behind a common patriotic front. Any fair estimate of these influences would show that Christians have contributed to national, cultural, and political life in far larger proportion than the size of their community would lead one to expect.

It must be admitted, however, that in the field of religious influence Eastern Christianity has fought a losing battle. Until comparatively modern days, the size of the indigenous Christian communities has steadily dwindled. Every year sees losses to Islam and no compensating addition from Muslim conversions. It is difficult to determine exactly the time at which the "until-then" Christian portions of the Muslim empire became a minority; certainly it was several centuries after Arab conquests. As noted earlier, the picture of the conquering Muslim offering Islam in one hand and extermination in the other is not historical. Doubtless there were incidents of this kind, but the accession of the Christian population to the Muslim faith was not due primarily to the threat of the sword. It was a process of attrition, in which social pressure, community discrimination, desire for majority status, political careers, and genuine conviction all played their part. This can still be seen in a country like Egypt, where there is a small but steady trickle of Coptic conversions to Islam. Sometimes it is a Coptic boy who wants to marry a Muslim girl, sometimes an ambitious leader who sees that the higher reaches of political or business life will be open to him only as a Muslim. Since conversion from Islam to Christianity is legally difficult and brings no social rewards, there are almost never Muslims who make up for this loss by becoming Coptic Christians.

To appreciate fully the problem of Christian religious influence in the Middle East, the particular legal and historical relations between the Christian and Muslim communities must be understood. First is the status of Christianity as a tolerated faith. Muhammad considered the Jews and Christians of his day as part of the monotheistic tradition that he held to be divinely ordained and originally revealed to the ancient prophets. He believed that these communities had adulterated the purity of that tradition by adding untrue doctrine (such as the divinity of Jesus) and altering the sacred Scripture, but he commanded that their religious life should be respected. In theory, though not always in fact, this meant that Muslim governments guaranteed the rights of the Christians under their rule to follow their traditional faith—as long as they did not proselytize the Muslim community. That was legally forbidden and still is, wherever *Sharia* (Muslim law) is strictly enforced.

Despite their tolerated status in the Muslim community, the Christians held a second-class citizenship. Until the rise of modern national states, for example, they did not serve in the conquering armies of the various Islamic empires. To compensate the state for this indulgence, Christians paid additional taxes. Sometimes, under fanatical rulers, they were forbidden to enter certain professions and enjoy privileges reserved for Muslims—such as riding a horse instead of a mule. Occasionally they were made to wear distinctive dress.

The modern national states of the Middle East have repudiated these medieval arrangements. Christians serve with Muslims in the armed forces and no legal disabilities to professions, social standing, dress, or employment exist. But neither the Muslim nor the Christian can escape from the long ages of the past, when to be a Christian was to hold a different relation to the national community than that held by the Muslim. Discriminatory practices in employment are widespread under those national laws that prescribe to all companies a certain percentage of indigenous employees. A company that has too large a proportion of Christians among its nationals may be frankly told that it ought to employ more Muslims. And while a few Christians may rise to the rank of cabinet minister, their appointment is on a basis of community representation rather than on sheer merit. To be a Christian in the Middle East is still to be a member of a community that is not expected to expand and that must be content to "keep its place" as a minority group. Even where conversion is legally recognized, it is often almost impossible to accomplish since the Muslim community still does not admit nor accept the *right* of a Muslim to change his faith.

Moreover, since the Muslim community is governed under *Sharia,* which is not applicable to other religious communities, non-Muslims are considered separate legal entities within the mechanism of government. This system is called the *millet* system, the *millet* being the religious community organized as a legal entity within the state. Each recognized church body (Coptic, Orthodox, Roman Catholic) has its community court that administers the community laws regarding personal status—marriage, divorce, inheritance. The leaders of the community (patriarch or council) have legal responsibilities to the government—and the government to them. When, after World War II, Ethiopia repudiated a centuries old custom of accepting as head of the Ethiopian Church an Egyptian nominated by the Coptic Patriarch of Egypt, the Egyptian government protested what it considered the loss of rights of one of its religious *millets*.

Under such a system, any change in faith also means a change in the legal status of the convert. It is not merely a matter of accepting one set of religious beliefs for another, but of appearing before a different court to be judged by different laws. And when a religious community has not been recognized by the government (as was often the case with Protestants in the early days of missionary work), the convert must continue either to be legally a member of his old community or have no legal rights in those matters with which the religious courts deal.

This system is on the way out in some parts of the Middle East. Under Turkey's program of secularization, the principle of religion as a legal denominator was abandoned (including the *millet* court system) in favor of European civil law. In 1955 Egypt abolished its *millet* courts, but not the principle of religious community law, which will still be applied by the civil courts according to the faith of the litigants. The Christian community has strongly resisted this change, partly because it is interpreted as a loss of religious prerogative, partly in fear that the civil law in a predominantly Muslim country will be permeated by Muslim feeling and principles.

Another factor that affects the Muslim-Christian relationship is the post-Christian birth of Islam and its conscious repudiation of the Christianity represented by Eastern churches. In Hindu, Buddhist, Confucian, or Shinto communities, Christianity comes as a young and foreign faith with which the religious consciousness of the inhabitants has little or no historical connection. On the other hand, although claiming to stand in the succession of the prophets, Muhammad rejected the Christian life he knew and presented Islam as a correction of its errors. The Koran, well-spring of Muslim faith, denies the crucifixion of Jesus and his divine character. It also makes belief in the Trinity the greatest of sins—*shirk* or "ascribing a partner to God." Thus Christianity is a familiar and false story to the Muslim. And the Eastern churches that surround him are both remnants and symbols of that story; their ikon worship, ancient rites, and "nonsense theology" (as one Muslim described it) are the very things from which Islam called mankind. Moreover, it was from these very churches that many Muslim converts were gained in the expansive days of the faith. As some Christians look upon the synagogue and Judaism as unenlightened holdovers from the past, so Muslims regard the ancient Eastern churches as survivals of an outmoded way that Islam banished thirteen centuries ago. In these circumstances, it is not strange that the Muslim community has seldom turned to Christian thought and practice in the Middle East with inquiry or interest. "What is past is dead," says a much quoted Arab proverb, and the age of Eastern Christianity, being past, is dead for most Muslims.

In theory, Western Christianity, especially Protestantism, ought to be equally dead. It espouses the same fundamental doctrines of Atonement, Incarnation, and Trinity that Muhammad rejected. In theological content, it is no more palatable to the Muslim than Eastern Orthodoxy. Yet in practice, Western Christian faith has influenced the Muslim Middle East at many points. It has been the bearer of modern education and social ideas. The Protestant or Roman Catholic missionary was never simply a Christian; he was always a *Western* Christian, carrying with him the fresh and modern outlook of the Western world as well as the gospel. Often the Muslim community was willing to run the risk of missionary religious influence in order to avail itself of the medicine, schools, orphanages, science, and social welfare that the missionary brought. More than that, in bringing these things, the missionary identified his kind of Christianity with progress and social concern—two things that Eastern religion, both Muslim and Christian, seldom included.

But Protestantism brought another value—the need for and possibility of religious reform. In repudiating medieval Roman Catholicism, the Protestant repudiated some of the outward marks of historic Christian faith that gave offence to the Muslim. The use of statues and ikons in the churches, the magical conception of the Mass, the adoration of the Virgin Mary as the "Mother of God," the crucifix with the suffering Christ—these often confirmed the Muslim's belief that Christianity was crude and idolatrous. When the Protestant abolished these from his worship and made it clear that they were not necessary nor central to Christian faith, he presented a view of religion that frequently found sympathy from the Muslim.

Protestantism's recapturing of the personal dedication of the individual to a life of free religious thought also had its appeal. The Protestant sought to cleanse Christianity of its accretions from Roman and medieval days and to return to the origins of his faith. In the same way, Muslims who are troubled by the seeming inadequacies of Islam in the modern world hope to maintain the pristine Muslim faith while repudiating much of the medieval theology and social custom in which it has been clothed. One of the by-products of the missionary school is the Muslim whose own religious faith has been quickened by contact with Christianity—quickened and altered by the personal, ethical, reforming spirit he met there. "What we need," more than one thoughtful Muslim has said, "is a reformation such as you had in Christianity."

The success of Protestant missions in winning converts from Islam in the Middle East has been slight. The Evangelical churches of the Middle East are composed mainly of Christians who have left their ancient communions to become Protestants. Every mission area has some examples, often noble ones, of Muslims who have withstood social pressure and personal danger to become Christians, but nowhere have there been such mass movements as in India or Africa.

If the Christian communities of the Middle East are to be judged on the quantitative basis of the number of conversions from Islam, they would have to admit failure. But while the spread of the faith through conversion is an inescapable obligation and opportunity, there are other obligations and opportunities that must not be underrated. One of these is witness, and it is here that Eastern Christianity has acquitted itself with honor. Through long centuries of minority status in the midst of a monolithic, non-Christian religious and social order, it has steadfastly kept the faith. Another obligation is service. Here Western Christianity has had its deepest impact. The Middle East has never known such an outpouring of concern for and service to human need as has come with the Christian gospel through the missionary movement. Whatever problems the Muslim world of the future may hold for the stubborn remnants of Christianity, the way of Christian witness and Christian service will be open.

3

Challenge to Faith

¶ TWO books were published in Cairo in 1950-51 that stirred bitter public debate. The first, called in English *From Here We Start,* was a devastating attack on traditional Islamic institutions and leadership, which were represented as barriers to national and social progress. The second, *The Beginning of Wisdom,* was an angry rejoinder, defending the faith from the "error and nonsense" of the attacker. This latter book claimed that traditional Islam was "designed to serve as a basis upon which a just, righteous, and charitable state could be founded."

This was not the first time, of course, that religion has been attacked and defended in the Middle East. Through the centuries Islam's personal ethic and prescribed piety have sat lightly upon some, as witness the convivial Omar Khayyam. Muslim theologians, too, have fought over the formulation of their faith with all the fury of medieval philosophers. Christian apologists, ancient and modern, have carried on a running argument with Islam, criticizing both its religious claims and moral values. Yet the Cairo attack and defense were different. Both books were written by orthodox Muslim professors within the walls of al-Azhar, the Muslim world's oldest and most venerated theological seminary. Both were concerned with the total claims of religion rather than of individual and debatable doctrines. And both evaluated Islam in terms of its effectiveness in the life of the community.

The problem these books consider from their opposite directions is a familiar one. In the East as in the West, modern man cannot escape the challenge our revolutionary times bring to the traditional claims of religion. That challenge is rooted in the profound social, political, and economic changes that are transforming world society. In this bewildering and unstable era, the question is, "Can religion reorganize life and give direction to these explosive forces?" A leading Protestant theologian, Walter Horton, asks, "Can Christianity save civilization?" The Muslim authors of these controversial books are asking a similar question in terms of their more limited problem, "Can historic Islam build the new society that the modern day is forcing on the Middle East?"

This question confronts both the political leaders and religious thinkers of Muslim lands. For the past century and a half, the disturbing and explosive forces of modernity have been penetrating the Middle East. Varied changes that the West took four centuries to absorb have been compressed into half that time in the Middle East. Ever since Napoleon first landed in Egypt in 1798, bringing with him the disturbing, if faint, echoes of the French Revolution, change has been inescapable. With accelerating rapidity, the radical innovations of the Western world have poured into the Middle East until today the old wineskins heave and creak with the swelling of the new wine. They must either contain it or burst in the attempt.

The tension between tradition and modernity produces changes that are both gradual and diffuse, but the abolition of the caliphate in 1922 stands as the measure of the altered role of religion in the Middle East.

As "Commander of the Faithful" the caliph was considered the secular head of the world Muslim community, following in the footsteps of Muhammad as a political leader. (Caliph means "follower.") Although the actual power of the caliph as the chief of state largely disappeared with the decline of the Arab Empire, the title continued as a symbol of the universal community of Islam. With the creation of the Ottoman Empire, the Turkish sultans adopted the title of "caliph" and thus laid claim to the religious loyalty of their Muslim subjects. At the outbreak of World War I, this claim was repudiated by non-Turkish Muslims when the Sultan called for a jihad against the Allies. Put to the test against the forces of modern nationalism, the caliphate proved to be an empty shell.

Four years after the war, the new Turkey abolished the office of caliph. This was done as part of the program for a Western-oriented, republican state, but its implications reached far beyond the borders of Turkey to the ends of the Muslim world. The caliphate was Islam's most venerable institution, the symbol of its religiously derived political authority. Yet when it was done away with, no serious attempt was made to restore it! Muslim rulers discussed the possibility on several occasions, but the political pre-eminence the title of caliph would give to a single ruler was unacceptable to the nationalistic Islamic states. Today Islam exists only as the established religion of separate governments, not as the supranational community of the faithful that it was originally designed to be.

Although the permanent disappearance of the caliphate is a dramatic and explicit change in the pattern of Islam in the Middle East, it is not a unique nor isolated occurrence. In almost every country the form of government, the basis of law, and the practices of society—all existing in the past as Islamic institutions—are being changed. There are still countries like Saudi Arabia, Yemen, and Afghanistan where religious law is paramount, and in every country there are sections of society who live by traditional religious practices. But on the frontiers of conflict between the modern world and medievalism, religion is openly or tacitly given second place as the determining factor in society. The call to prayer still sounds from slender minarets across the crowded bazaars and earnest groups still chant their ancient rites in unobtrusive little churches, but neither the traditional church nor the traditional mosque seems likely to determine the future—or even the present.

How does the Middle East try to reconcile the tension between its historic faith and the demands of the new age? One answer is in the adoption of secularism, by which parts of personal and corporate life are removed from the sphere of religion and assigned to nonreligious state control. The extreme example of this is Turkey. A philospher of the revolution stated the aims of the new Turkish orientation as (1) nationalism, to develop the intellectual forces slumbering in the Turkish people, (2) Europeanism, based on the acceptance of the civilization of the modern West, and (3) religious reform, or a return to the intellectual content and spirit of true Islam, which was viewed as a collection of spiritual—not political—principles. In practice, this program meant adoption of a republican form of government, abolition of religious law in personal and civil procedures, adoption of monogamy, curtailment of the privileges of the clergy, discontinuance of the teaching of religion in state schools, and abolition of the *millet* system. Religion remained as the private concern of indivduals and not as the arbiter of social and political practices. To most of the rest of the Muslim world, this seemed a great betrayal, equivalent to a complete repudiation of Islam. For Turkey it was the prerequisite for rebirth in the modern world.

No other Middle Eastern state has adopted secularization as completely or openly as Turkey. Reza Shah, the "Ataturk" of Iran, also tried to secularize the life of his country. He did succeed in limiting the power of the religious leaders and he introduced many changes on the Turkish pattern, but Islam still remains a powerful force among the common people. However, in practice the government of Iran is guided more by secular than by religious considerations, although the façade of a religious society still persists. It is remarkable that in many Iranian programs of social development no reference is made to religion and there is little attempt to utilize religious institutions as a social force.

There has been no comparable adoption of the theory of the secular state in the Arab world, although the Egyptian revolution of 1951 shows some aspects of the Turkish pattern. Islam, after all, is an integral part of the political history of the Arab people, whereas it came to Iran and Turkey as a foreign innovation. Turkish nationalism can appeal to pre-Islamic "Turanianism" in criticism of the Muslim system, and Iran can recall the splendor of Darius the Great. But when the Arab, under the spell of his new nationalism, turns to his past, he finds only an Islamic era in which religion was the substance and form of political power. Islam first brought the Arabs out of their desert sands to become a great people, and every modern national movement among the Arabs (except the Christian Lebanese) tends to reactivate Muslim consciousness.

Nevertheless, the modern states of Egypt, Syria, Iraq, and Jordan have adopted essentially non-Islamic forms of government, inspired by the secular examples of the Western world. All these states have some form of constitutional monarchy or parliamentary republic, copied after European practices in which religion plays a minor role. Islam is still the established religion of the state, as Orthodoxy was in Czarist Russia, but its practical responsibilities are limited to the religious courts that govern matters of personal status. In civil and criminal law, the Napoleonic Code or the Swiss Law Code, which are basically nonreligious in character and application, have replaced *Sharia*. Citizenship is based on birth rather than membership in a religious community and all citizens pay equal taxes and serve in the armed forces. Social and economic legislation is drawn more from the practices of the Western world than from Islamic teaching and institutions. The practical secularization of Islamic life is proceeding in the Arab world, although there is no official separation between mosque and state as in Turkey. Perhaps this apparent inconsistency in approach is most obvious in Pakistan. This state calls itself an "Islamic republic," yet in practice it is far more secular than many of the "democracies" of the Arab world that reject the term "Islamic" in describing themselves.

Modernism has not only produced a movement toward political secularism but it has also invaded Muslim religious thought. Modernism seeks a reinterpretation of Islam that holds fast to essential faith, yet makes room for the innovations of the modern age. Significantly, the movement did not begin as the result of scientific discovery and advancement.

Rather, it was an attempt to reshape Islam after Western contact had revealed the political and cultural weakness of the Middle East. The successive defeats of the disintegrating Turkish Empire, the British occupation of Egypt, the Anglo-Russian pressure on Iran and Afghanistan before World War I, all shocked and humiliated Muslim feeling. In seeking a reason for this helplessness in the face of the modern world, some thinkers blamed the outworn institutions of medieval Islam. One notable reformer, Sheikh Ali Abd el Razzak of Egypt, wrote: "There is nothing in Islam to prevent Muslims from tearing down that ancient order under which they have been subjugated and under which they have been humbled, and from building up the rule of their kingdoms and the order of their governments upon the most recent conclusions arrived at by the minds of man." In practical application of this view, he attacked the caliphat since "we have no need of this caliphate, either in the affairs of our religious life or in those of our civil life. For the caliphate has always been, and continues to be, a misfortune to Islam and to Muslims, and a source of evil and corruption." To support this radical departure from Muslim traditionalism, the sheikh redefined Muhammad's mission, maintaining that the divine law was only concerned with religious affairs, never with secular. Under such terms, the caliphate rested upon a mistaken conception of the Prophet's purpose.

The earliest prominent figure in this movement was Jamal el Din el Afghani, who, in the middle of the nineteenth century, passed like a burning brand across the Middle East, kindling fires of dissatisfaction and hope wherever he went. At various times he was expelled from or "permitted to leave" Afghanistan, India, Persia, Egypt, and Turkey because the radical reforms he proposed seemed to menace religious faith and political stability. Jamal el Din believed external reforms in his medieval society should be carried out by force—a view adopted decades later by Ataturk. But he also believed that true Islam, rightly understood, was an essential of national regeneration. A Sufi mystic, he repudiated much of the social and political trappings of Islam while clinging to its inner and spiritual force.

Jamal el Din's Egyptian disciple, Sheikh Muhammad Abdu, was an even more potent force in the modernist movement. First as a lecturer at al-Azhar, then as the chief legal leader (mufti) of Egypt, he was able to introduce significant educational reforms. Although his actual achievements in changing the teaching methods and curriculum at al-Azhar now seem modest, they marked the beginning of a new day in the education of Muslim leaders. One of Muhammad Abdu's basic principles was to compare early Islamic practices with the many institutions that had been absorbed into the Muslim system at a later time. Claiming for modern thinkers the same freedom of interpretation that was exercised by the first four caliphs (the "Rightly Guided Ones"), he propounded a series of legal decisions that radically differed from historic Muslim practice—such as permitting Muslims to accept interest on postal savings deposits or allowing them to eat meat killed by Christians. Although he left no systematic commentary on the Koran, his reinterpretation of koranic texts and the principles he applied have become the basis of much modern Muslim thought.

It was one of Muhammad Abdu's disciples, Taha Husain, an Egyptian, who carried this approach to its logical conclusion through applying the methods of modern historical criticism to the Koran itself. Taha Husain is one of the most remarkable thinkers in the Arab world. Blind from early childhood, he was first trained at al-Azhar under Muhammad Abdu. "Why," he asked as a young man, "should I simply repeat what the ancients said—why should I spend my life in praising the orthodox Sunnites or berating the heretical Shiites?" His inquiring spirit led him to Paris and Sorbonne University, where he was introduced to modern studies and immersed in Gallic clarity that ever since have deeply influenced his writings. Even his language exhibits the logical simplicity of the French that is quite foreign to the involved and ornate style of much classical Arabic.

Taha Husain questioned whether the famed pre-Islamic "Suspended Poems" (Muallaqat) were really original, suggesting that they had been created in later times to justify certain grammatical usages in the Koran.

He also cast doubt on the strict historicity of some of the Koran's leading figures—notably Moses; his contention being that the religious lessons drawn from Moses' life would be true even if Moses himself had never lived. Such startling suggestions outraged Muslim leaders, and Dr. Husain was dismissed from his government post and exiled from many Muslim intellectual circles. It is hard to be a prophet in the wilderness, and in later years, while still a champion of liberal causes, Taha Husain has moderated his views—or at least not talked about them so much.

Another significant modernist was Sir Muhammad Iqbal, the spiritual leader and philosopher of those Muslim movements in India that created Pakistan. Deeply committed to modern science, he wrote in one of his poems that the "progress of the West comes neither from the sound of the lute nor the dancing of maidens unveiled. It is from science and art that its lamp has been lighted." To light this lamp for Islam, Muhammad Iqbal proposed a radical reconstruction of Muslim philosophy—the only truly inclusive philosophic system modernism has produced. He contended that the Koran was given as a guide through the period when modern science was unknown. With the creation of that science, the task of intellectual discovery must be done by scientific methods, not by reference to Koranic authority. Since both the Koran and science were given by God as guides to men, one did not contradict the other; the Koran performed its task by leading men to the threshold of the modern world and science took up the task from there. This is almost the reverse of the Christian view of Thomas Aquinas that scientific knowledge leads man to the threshold of faith and faith then reveals what science cannot know.

In some form, such modernist views have permeated the new intellectuals of the Muslim Middle East, especially the student groups, but it is hard to speak of a true modernist "movement" among them. One reason is that the forces of modernism have remained individual, scattered, and unorganized in the face of traditionalism. There is no theological seminary of modernist views to counter the influence of such institutions as al-Azhar. When a public outcry is raised against some bold innovation in Islamic thought, the forces of traditionalism in government and mosque are not countered by a modernist organization that knits together the influence and impact of liberal scholars. To be an open and bold liberal is still a lonely business. Modernism spreads much more as a general atmosphere of thought than as a well defined movement openly advocating a reinterpretation of historic faith.

There is, however, a deeper reason why modernism finds itself confused and impeded. To carry out its task of intellectual reconstruction, as Taha Husain saw, the Koran itself must be critically examined. Much of the political and social structure of medieval Islam claims the authority of the Prophet's own practice and his legislation on community affairs as contained in Koranic verses. If a new political and social system, based on Western practices, is to be adopted, a distinction must be made between the *social* content of the Koran and its *spiritual* teachings. The first needs to be recognized as temporal, reflecting the conditions of seventh century Arabia; the latter, as eternal truth applicable to every generation. Such a treatment of the Koran, however, runs counter to Islam's conviction that its Scripture is completely and verbally inspired in all its parts and all its teachings. For the Muslim to question the authority of the Koran is as serious and disturbing as for the Christian to question the divinity of Christ. This is because the final authority of Islam is a book, not a person, and to question that book shakes faith to its foundations. On the other hand, the final authority of the Christian is not the Bible, but the Incarnation, which is the living Word of God and the revelation of his character and purpose. Until Muslim thought can accept certain parts of the Koran as only temporarily relevant to the day in which they were written, it will be impossible to reconcile its traditional faith with the demands of the new age.

It is natural that in opposition to secularism and modernism, there should be a resurgence of traditional religion in the Middle East. Traditionalists attempt to reinstate Islam as a definitive political and social force, although the Islam to be reinstated is frequently tinged with new or reforming ideas. Best known is the Wahhabi movement of Arabia, which is Islamic puritanism in its most extreme form. This movement, launched in central Arabia in the eighteenth century, bases its practices only on the Koran and the earliest traditions and discards the theological and legal elaboration of later centuries. It forbids the cult of the saints, the use of tobacco, excessive luxury in dress, and the use of speculative reason as an instrument for elaborating religious truth. In theory it is a kind of Protestantism—an attempt to return to the earliest days of the faith and accept nothing but what is found there. Modern Saudi Arabia is Wahhabi oriented. Although Saudi Arabia is still ruled by Koranic law and embodies traditional ideas of a Muslim state (the Muslim Creed appears on the national flag), it has had to come to terms with such innovations as the telephone, motor cars, and modern schools. Wahhabi prohibitions on music, the arts, liquor, and tobacco are observed, however, and the penalty for proven theft is still the amputation of the offending hand, as ordered in the Koran.

Obviously such stern puritanism is not likely to appeal to more modern parts of the Middle East. Wahhabism has not spread outside the Arabian Peninsula, although there are traditionalist movements in other countries that are similarly dedicated to a return to the Muslim state. The one best known to the West, perhaps, is the Muslim Brotherhood. This movement began before World War II. Led by an organizer of remarkable ability, it evolved a political program aimed at re-establishing the state as a Muslim institution, although along somewhat modern lines. After the war and in connection with the struggle over Palestine, the Brotherhood emerged with considerable power, particularly in Egypt. It had its own newspaper and a large following in the villages, and was responsible for the assassination of two highly placed Egyptian officials. For a time the Muslim Brotherhood represented a very serious problem to the country. Although some of the officers in Nasser's revolutionary movement were suspected of having been members of the Brotherhood, the new government gradually pushed the Brotherhood out of political life, making an attempt to murder Nasser the occasion for smashing the organization's leadership. For a time, the Brotherhood spread its movement to Iraq, Jordan, and Syria, but its real strength had been in Egypt.

There have been other similar movements on a smaller scale. During Mossadegh's regime in Iran, the "Devoted Ones of Islam" under the leadership of Mullah Kashani exercised brief political influence. Sporadically there have been youth movements in Arab countries, such as "The Young Men of Muhammad" and the "Green Shirts" (green is the traditional Muslim color). Each of these has used religion as the rallying point of political action and called for a return to the Muslim pattern of the past. For all their political expediency, they are witnesses to a desire to find some specifically *Muslim* pattern for their national progress.

Here is the unsolved problem that the modern challenge of faith brings to the Middle East. On one hand there is an impressive, ancient, and deeply rooted religious system and experience that is native to the area and has guided its life for thirteen centuries. On the other, there is the inescapable pressure of the modern world and the urgent desire to shake off the reproach of backwardness. Secularism, as practiced in the West, does not satisfy, for it too easily destroys the spiritual basis of life. Religious traditionalism would lead the Muslim world back to a past that is gone forever. Between the two, sincere men of faith are looking for some way by which they can be true to their heritage, yet fully a part of the modern world.

4

The Good to Be Done

¶ AMERICAN Protestant Christianity began missionary work in the Middle East on January 14, 1820. On that day, Pliny Fisk and Levi Parsons disembarked at Smyrna, Turkey, as the pioneer representatives of the American Board of Commissioners for Foreign Missions to the "Jews . . . pagans . . . Mohammedans . . . Christians, the people of Palestine, Egypt, Syria, Armenia."

Their instructions were phrased in surprisingly generous terms. "The two grand enquiries ever present in your minds," they were told, "will be 'what good can be done?' and 'by what means?'" The absence of more specific directions to evangelize and convert was not because their sponsoring missionary society lacked a commitment to the direct witness of the Christian gospel, but because the area was so new and their vision of Christian service so broad that they were willing to leave to missionaries the task of finding the appropriate method of Christian testimony.

In the years of Christian effort that followed, these original instructions have been given a content far beyond the vision of their authors. While the missionary movement necessarily has embraced a wide variety of religious convictions and differing definitions of Christian activity, the "good to be done" and the "means of doing it" have been imaginative and varied. Today there are over fifteen hundred Protestant missionaries in the lands of the Middle East, representing over eighty different world organizations. Their work has included almost every phase of human service—schools, universities, orphanages, literacy campaigns, hospitals, agricultural demonstrations, churches.

Such a record of service has been warmly recognized, even by those who do not accept its religious objectives. Many Muslims are deeply grateful for the missionaries' contributions in the field of health, education, and social service, even if they fail to accept the Christian message as the result of these activities. Foreigners, too, have recognized the missionaries' dispassionate zeal, which set a high standard of rectitude.

However impressive this record of service and witness, like every other activity in the Middle East, it faces a new era with new problems. As the latter part of this book has made clear, the most significant aspect of the Middle East today is not its unchanging past, but its changing future. No facet of life is untouched by the currents of the modern world. Politics, society, international relations, business practices—and faith—are all in tension between yesterday and tomorrow and the only thing that can be said with surety is that tomorrow will be different from today. It is this fact that challenges the Christian world to return again to the missionary directive of 1820 and ask, "In the Middle East of today, what is the good to be done and by what means can it be achieved?"

The inquiry cannot be fully answered. As Parsons and Fisk had to evolve a program of Christian work out of their experience in the old Middle East so it is only by contemporary experience in the new and changing Middle East that the shape and content of the future Christian task will be determined. Yet in closing this brief study of Middle Eastern lands, the Christian with world concern must ponder some basic aspects of the missionary situation as it appears today.

The first is that the Christian enterprise appears in a dual role to Eastern eyes. It is Christian, based upon and devoted to a religious message that we believe to be timeless in its truth and universal in its applicability. But it is also Western. The Christian message comes to the East embodied in a Western movement. It is never simply a Christian missionary who witnesses and works among Muslims. It is always a Western (American, British, Continental) Christian witnessing to and working among Eastern (Egyptian, Palestinian, Iranian) Muslims. To the natural tensions that have always existed between the Christian and Muslim religious systems, there are added the problems and resentments that grow out of East-West international relationships. The fact that the missionary movement is Christian and the fact that it is Western are equally important in determining what the Christian task is and how it will be received by those it touches.

Of these two relationships, it is clearly the Western character of the Christian enterprise that has commended missionary work to the Middle East in the past. The missionary was usually accepted, not because he was a Christian but because he was a Westerner, identified with a culture and technical services that the Middle East increasingly desired. Indeed, the missionary was one of the earliest and most ubiquitous representatives of the social and humanitarian programs of the Western world in the Middle East. He gave many communities their first experience of modern medicine, education, and social work.

Examples of this and of its lasting contribution to the Middle East are numerous. An Iranian's response to the United States program of technical assistance (Point Four) in his country was, "Yes, it's a good thing—but not new. This is what the missionaries have been doing here for several decades." The impressive development of Kuwait under its present ruler, using his vast resources of oil royalties, was in a measure due to almost fifty years of missionary work that had implanted in the ruling family the values of schools and hospitals. Generations of Middle Eastern students first found in Christian schools a vision of social service. One Muslim doctor opened a free clinic for the poor and when asked why he did so, answered, "I went to a missionary school and ever since have been uncomfortable in the face of human need."

Yet this very Western character of Christian activity, which was such an asset in the past, is today becoming a serious liability. Partly as a result of missionary work, partly from increasing contact with the Western world, Middle Eastern governments are rapidly developing their own national programs of social betterment. Western institutions (whether Christian or secular) often are viewed as rivals to this effort or as foreign intrusions into the prerogatives and responsibilities of the state.

Moreover, the political relations between the Middle East and the Western world have changed radically. When missionary endeavor first started, both the culture and political power of the Middle East were decadent and the intrusion of the West could not have been prevented even had there been a national consciousness to fight against it. But today the newly formed, or reborn, states of the Middle East, still smarting with resentment and frustration from the years of Western domination, demand equality in international relations. Since this clashes with the need of the West to continue effective influence in a critical cold war area, the Middle East is in increasing conflict with the very countries from which the missionary movement is launched.

This situation not only conditions the character and program of future Christian missionary effort, but in itself presents a major challenge to Christians of the Western world. For while we recognize that there will probably never be such a thing as a "Christian" foreign policy or a "Christian" international world, we equally recognize that our faith is concerned with the relation between people in its most inclusive sense.

The Middle East is not only a problem as an area in which to bear Christian witness. It is also a problem as to how the formerly dominant Western powers are to relate themselves to the rising self-consciousness and independence of peoples they long controlled. Since World War II, a series of crises have given testimony to the depth and acceleration of this problem. The nationalization of British owned oil operations in Iran, the violent reaction of the Arab world to the creation of Israel, the nationalization of the Suez Canal, the growing alignment of Syria and Egypt with the Soviet Union—all these are facets in the struggle of the Middle East to achieve what it believes to be a more acceptable pattern of international relations.

Can the Christian forces of the West play a role in offsetting or mediating such political difficulties? Certainly in the past the work of many individual missionaries embodied a highly developed concept of East-West relationships. Outside the missionary movement, most of the Westerners who came to the Middle East did so with one of two objectives: to exercise political control as the representative of a Western power; or to develop commercial enterprises. These are the two historic instruments of international relations. Great nations whose interests are involved in small nations (and the West's destiny in the modern world has always been involved in the Middle East) tried either to control the small nations politically or to trade with them. Both methods are necessary and inescapable—and, in the hands of their best leaders, have contributed to much human good. But both have in them the seeds of rivalry and tension, as the modern history of the Middle East only too well illustrates.

What the missionary has done—imperfectly, it is true—is to introduce a different kind of relation between East and West. This has been a relationship built on the recognition of human need and the accompanying desire to meet that need, simply because it is human. Not all missionaries have consciously followed this vision, but where it is found it is an important aspect of Christian influence. The mission hospital is not simply a device to interest sick people in the gospel through rendering them a service. It is also an expression of relatedness between the medical science of the West and the needy people of the East. Born out of Christian compassion and concern, it seeks no political or economic reward in return for its presence.

Can this spirit be embodied in new and more effective instruments today? Certainly there are still areas where Christian organizations can render unique service in this spirit. An example is the work done among the Palestinian refugees by Church World Service, the Y.M.C.A., and other Christian-motivated organizations. This service is rendered without any commitment to the political issues of the tragic and difficult situation. It is an expression of a non-political Western concern for the desperate needs of desperate people. But may it not be possible for Christian forces to render an even larger service? Because Christians are identified neither with Jewish faith nor Arab feeling, there is the possibility that they might serve as a stimulus to quiet mediation in this difficult area. At least Christian leaders should consider such a role and attempt to sound more deeply the minds of the contending parties. The great fear of both Arab and Israeli is that current approaches to the refugee situation will involve political commitments that they cannot accept. Thus they view with suspicion every move to discuss the refugee problem, seeing behind it political motivations that experience has made them distrust. Might it not now be possible for Christian forces, disassociating themselves equally from the political interests of their own governments and the rival fears of the contending parties, to investigate how such a problem as this might be approached?

There is another important role of mediation that Christian service in the Middle East can perform. Of all Western movements in the area, it is missionary activity that has entered most deeply into the hopes and aspirations of the East. Because the missionary expects to spend his entire career in the area, he learns the language of the people and is devoted to a task that involves him in daily contact with their life and customs. This places the Christian representative in the Middle East in a unique position to interpret its life to the Western world. Such movements as nationalism, the struggle against Western colonialism, and the drive for economic self-determination have, on the whole, been understood and accepted more sympathetically by the missionary than by any other foreigner. At times this may irritate the Western administrator who is not dispassionate because of the very nature of his task. What he fails to realize and accept is that the missionary has entered so deeply into the situation that he understands it in terms of the local community as well as in terms of the policy that his own country may be pursuing.

To put it more simply: there are two sides to every question of East-West contacts, and when the missionary (consciously or unconsciously) speaks with sympathetic interpretation of the East he is doing both it and his own Western people an indispensable service.

While Christian activity cannot escape this "Western" role it is not, of course, the most basic concern. Missionary work can never be justified simply in terms of good will, for that good will is the product of a Christian dedication that is rooted in the personal acceptance of the Christian life. Whatever the Western missionary does, his task is indefensible and incomplete unless he always acts as a *Christian,* recognizing both his obligation and opportunity to witness to the claims of the gospel.

Here, too, there are problems peculiar to the Middle East. As we have already seen, there is a particular character to the historic Christian-Muslim relation, quite distinct from Christian-Hindu or Christian-Buddhist relationship. Christianity has not had the success in Muslim lands that it has had elsewhere, in part because the two faiths have long stood in conscious opposition to each other with Islam consistently repudiating the heart of Christian doctrine. Yet, despite indifference and hostility that has lasted through the centuries, Christian work in the Middle East has made a religious contribution over and above the actual winning of converts and the formation of the church.

Frequently the unconscious result of missionary endeavor has been to revitalize the faith of Muslims. The Protestant emphasis on personal religious experience, the criticism of religion as a formal exercise, the defense of Christian faith against the secular influences of materialism—these are often appropriated by Muslims and incorporated into their own religious life. It is not uncommon for thoughtful Muslims to speak of their need for a "reformation" in Islam. Indeed, in one Muslim country there has been a group which calls itself "Protestant Muslims."

Again the missionary has sharply emphasized the right of the individual to make his own religious choices. This is not a basic Muslim conception, for Islam (as we have seen) is not a personal but a communal faith and it is hard for Islam to recognize the right of the individual to embrace another faith that seems destructive to itself. This view is still strong in many Muslim countries, but the missionary is constantly raising the issue of personal freedom in religion.

Finally, the quickened ethical sense of modern Christianity, with its concern for current problems, has penetrated many Eastern minds. The Muslim and Eastern Christian ethical systems, as enshrined in their historic books, have little to say about such vital questions as modern war, industrial relations, major social reforms, and many aspects of the changing patterns of modern family life. While the general influence of Western thought inevitably raises these issues for the Muslim and Eastern Christian, mission activity has played an important role. By it the Middle Eastern mind has been stimulated to consider how its own religious heritage can serve the crucial issues of today. Often this involves the unconscious acceptance of modern Christian ethical standards.

This task is particularly urgent now, when the social and religious concepts of the Middle East are increasingly challenged by the disruptive forces of our own confused Western world. Especially is it vital as Russia penetrates the area. Whatever may be the immediate political policies of the Soviet Union, the only answers to social and national problems it brings are in terms of its own Communist doctrine and experience. Russia cannot be present politically in the Middle East for long without infecting the region with its anti-religious approach to life. All men of faith—whether Muslim or Christian—need to stand together before the onslaught. If the Christian mind of the West can help the Muslim mind of the East rediscover and defend the basically religious view of life, it will have performed an indispensable service.

Yet no Christian is content to stop short of a full and direct witness to the truth of the gospel. This is the area in which missionary activity has been least successful; the number of converts from Islam is small and the churches they form are weak and scattered. Of course there is no easy panacea that will either change the Muslims' long centuries of opposition to Christianity or attire Christianity itself with a new attractiveness making it readily acceptable to the Muslim mind. Yet there are aspects of the Christian witness that need to be soberly reconsidered.

One is the tendency to be negative—to attack Islam as a Christian rival rather than to present Christian faith positively and in its own relation to basic human problems. Much of the traditional missionary literature in the past has been of this controversial character and has naturally evoked Muslim attacks against Christian doctrine.

This situation is the result of long centuries of continued controversy and of the fact that Islam and Christianity are sharply opposed at certain vital points of doctrine. It is also the reflection of the "backward" social conditions in many Eastern lands, which the Christian compares unfavorably with the Western way of life, throwing on Islam the major blame. There is therefore a natural temptation to approach the Muslim in terms of what is wrong with his faith rather than to present him with the Christian way as a positive and universal life.

To bear positive witness means that the Christian message must be stated in terms of the modern concerns of the Middle East. Traditional Western theology often appears as incomprehensible and irrelevant to the modern Muslim as it does to many people in the West. This is not because it is untrue, but because it is stated in the thought patterns of a bygone age and does not always concern itself with the forms in which old problems return to modern men. One medical missionary with years of service in the Muslim world stated the task thus: "No one in Arabia needs to be saved from 'Mohammedanism'—any more than the New York businessman needs to be saved from his inherent Greek stoicism. What they both need to be saved from is their hates and fears, their sins and prides." The parallel is not exact, for while the businessman may not know he is a stoic, the Muslim certainly knows he is a *Muslim.* Yet to focus the gospel primarily on the needs of modern men rather than on the structure of their traditional faith is the prerequisite for making clear that now, as always, the gospel is indeed "the power of God unto salvation."

Another aspect of much Christian effort is the failure to understand the living values of Islam as well as its weaknesses and failures. Whatever criticism the Christian may level against Islam as a religious faith, clearly it has provided religious satisfaction and spiritual strength to many people through many centuries. What is the source of this strength? How do Muslim devotions satisfy man's need to worship God? In the day of discouragement and the hour of death, what is it in Islam that gives courage and strength? To what aspects of his faith does the modern Muslim turn when confronted with the problems of the modern world? Until such questions as these are investigated more deeply and sympathetically, the true nature of Islam will be misjudged and the spiritual content of the gospel will be difficult to present to Muslim believers. Certainly Muslim theology and philosophy need to be studied, but more than that, the faith in which the Muslim lives today must be understood. That faith is rooted in personal satisfactions that are tested by experience and it is these satisfactions the Christian must understand and appreciate if he is to assist in discovering the deeper answers of the gospel to human needs.

Finally, it can never be said too frequently that the ultimate resource of the Christian gospel is in the living witness of Christian communities and individual lives. When Western "Christian" nations and the churches within them appear complacent in the face of such social questions as racial discrimination, the Muslim world quickly reads a lesson in their weakness. In the midst of World War II an editorial written by a Muslim in a Beirut newspaper asked, "How can the bearers of the Cross celebrate the birthday of the Prince of Peace when their nations are tearing at each other's throats?"

This is not to say that there is no hope of commending Christianity to the Muslim world until our own civilization is perfectly Christian—else the task would be indefinitely postponed. But it does mean that the action of Christian people in the West is studied by Muslims in the East and the voice of the church on Western social problems is part of the missionary enterprise. More than this, the depth of spiritual life among Western Christians living in the Middle East is the faith's greatest resource. However much the opportunities to conduct schools or hospitals, to do street preaching, or to found churches may be restricted, there can be no restriction on the witness of Christian living. Whether as a diplomat, Point Four technician, oil well operator, or missionary, the Christian bears a witness through his living that no legislation can ever forbid.

When leaving the Middle East after twenty-five years of Christian service, the writer met with a group of Egyptian friends to seek their counsel as to what he should say after his return to America. All the burning political issues of the day were suggested—Israel, the Suez Canal, the cold war. Finally an older member of the circle broke in with some impatience to say, "Yes, all these are important. But there is something more important. When you return to America, please tell your friends that, however much they need our canals, oil wells, air fields, and defense pacts, we are more than these. Tell them, we are people!" Here spoke the most neglected, yet truest, fact of the area we have called *The Lands Between.* Geography, races, politics, religion—yes, but beyond all these, *people.* People like ourselves—stirred to deep restlessness by a confusing age, frustrated by forces from distant lands and strange people they cannot control, seeking that simple, human happiness that all men cherish. And people like ourselves who need fresh faith and spiritual renewal to play their role and find their peace in the strange, new world that has burst upon us all.

SELECTED READINGS

Friendship Press books may be ordered from denominational literature headquarters. Books of other publishers are listed as supplementary resources. The views expressed in them are not necessarily those of the author or publishers of *The Lands Between.*

FRIENDSHIP PRESS BOOKS

Baly, Denis. MULTITUDES IN THE VALLEY. Today's issues in the Palestinian area. Student edition, paper $2.25. Greenwich, Conn.: Seabury Press, 1958. Cloth, with illustrations, $5.00.

Blumberg, John. THIS IS THE MIDDLE EAST. A new addition to the pictorial "This Is" series. Paper only, 60 cents.

Geren, Paul. NEW VOICES, OLD WORLDS. Popularly written biographies of Middle East Christians. Cloth $2.95, paper $1.50.

Johnson, R. Park. MIDDLE EAST PILGRIMAGE. A comprehensive study that gives valuable insights into religious and secular forces at work in the area. Cloth $2.95, paper $1.50.

Harrison, Ann M. A TOOL IN HIS HAND. A biographical narrative of the achievements of a Christian doctor in Arabia. Cloth $2.95, paper $1.50.

Wilson, J. Christy. INTRODUCING ISLAM. Valuable new material has been added to bring this classic study up to date. Paper only, 60 cents.

Wysner, Glora. CAUGHT IN THE MIDDLE. The author stresses the problems of the Middle East youth as they seek a place in the changing world. Cloth $2.95, paper $1.50.

BOOKS OF OTHER PUBLISHERS

Middle East History, Politics, and Social Conditions

*Atiyah, Edward. THE ARABS. Baltimore, Md.: Penguin Books, Inc., 1955.

*Faris, N. A., and Husayn, M. T. THE CRESCENT IN CRISIS. Lawrence, Kan.: University of Kansas Press, 1955.

*Hitti, Philip K. THE ARABS: A SHORT HISTORY. Chicago: Gateway Editions, Inc., 1956.

*Kirk, George E. A SHORT HISTORY OF THE MIDDLE EAST. Washington, D. C.: Public Affairs Press, 1947.

* Marks the volumes which the author recommends as most helpful for those who must choose one or two books on each topic.

*Morrison, S. A. MIDDLE EAST TENSIONS. New York: Harper & Brothers, 1954.

Antonius, George. THE ARAB AWAKENING: THE STORY OF THE ARAB NATIONAL MOVEMENT. Philadelphia: J. B. Lippincott, 1939.

Elis, Harry B. ISRAEL AND THE MIDDLE EAST. New York: The Ronald Press Co., 1957.

Fisher, Sydney Nettleton. SOCIAL FORCES IN THE MIDDLE EAST. Ithaca, N. Y.: Cornell University Press, 1955.

Frye, Richard N. (ed.). THE NEAR EAST AND THE GREAT POWERS. Cambridge: Harvard University Press, 1951.

Hourani, A. H. MINORITIES IN THE ARAB WORLD. London: Oxford University Press, 1947.

Royal Institute of International Affairs. THE MIDDLE EAST: A POLITICAL AND ECONOMIC SURVEY, 2nd ed. London: Oxford University Press, 1955. (Third edition in preparation.)

Van Ess, John. MEET THE ARAB. New York: John Day, 1943.

Young, T. Cuyler (ed.). NEAR EASTERN CULTURE AND SOCIETY. Princeton: Princeton University Press, 1951.

Islam

*Cragg, Kenneth. THE CALL OF THE MINARET. New York: Oxford University Press, 1956.

*Guillaume, Alfred. ISLAM. Baltimore, Md.: Penguin Books, Inc., 1954.

Gibb, H. A. R. MODERN TRENDS IN ISLAM. Chicago: University of Chicago Press, 1947.

*Smith, Wilfred Cantwell. ISLAM IN MODERN HISTORY. Princeton, N. J.: Princeton University Press, 1957.

Christian History and Missionary Development

*Addison, James Thayer. THE CHRISTIAN APPROACH TO THE MOSLEM. New York: Columbia University Press, 1942.

Calverley, Elinor T. MY ARABIAN DAYS AND NIGHTS: A MEDICAL MISSIONARY IN OLD KUWAIT. New York: Thomas Y. Crowell, 1958.

Latourette, Kenneth Scott. A HISTORY OF CHRISTIANITY. New York: Harper & Brothers, 1953.

Rasooli, Jay M. and Allen, Cady H. DR. SA'EED OF IRAN. Grand Rapids, Mich.: Grand Rapids International Publications, 1957.

INDEX